The Happy Expat

Your Guide to *Joyfully* Retiring Abroad

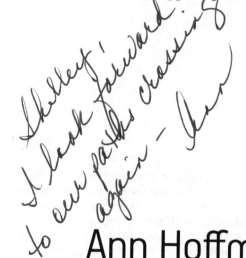

Ann Hoffman

M⊙tivational® **PRESS**
LEADERS IN GLOBAL PUBLISHING

Published by Motivational Press, Inc.
1777 Aurora Road
Melbourne, Florida, 32935
www.MotivationalPress.com

Manufactured in the United States of America.

ISBN: 978-1-62865-227-7

This book is dedicated to You,
Because you dare to dream

CONTENTS

ACKNOWLEDGEMENTS

ACKNOWLEDGEMENTS ARE KIND OF TRICKY. WHAT IF I FORGET someone? What if I include someone who doesn't want to be mentioned by name? A bit of a murky pond. So I decided I would just do it my way and whoever decides to be offended, so be it. (Learning that one can't please everyone is so freeing!)

I begin with my parents, Myron and Maxine (and don't panic, this won't be an endless list). We moved a lot because my dad was in the Army and my folks made it fun. This gave me a taste for travel and exploring the unknown. It has served me well.

Next up are the folks whom I could tell thought I was probably jousting at windmills. They kept me inspired, if for no other reason than to prove to them and, more importantly, to myself, that I really am able to go the distance. And I did!

Tamela Buhrke has been with me through thick and thin. She has been as enthusiastic for my success as I've been, sometimes even more when I found myself doubting if I could do this. This book would not exist if not for her continual contributions to it.

I am eternally grateful to Debbie, Sue and the rest of the gang at La Dolce Vita coffee shop. They are to be commended for keeping me in coffee and sandwiches throughout this endeavor and letting me take over one of their tables, use their wi-fi, and otherwise hang out.

Next is the woman who has kept me focused and on target with not only this book, she has kept me focused on putting all the pieces in place for other parts of my life as well. Lorna DiMeo is an extraordinary person who also has an incredible gift of singing. Not just any singing – she sings to the essence of a person, giving what is needed in that moment. I asked her to create a Power Song for me (I know, I know, sounds woo woo and is definitely not, there's data to back it up). When I play that song at least once in a day I really want to crank, I am able to elevate my work to a much higher level than anticipated. For example, I planned to outline one chapter of this book, played my Song, and proceeded to outline the entire book in about two hours. So thank you, Lorna, for all that you have given me. (If you'd like her to help you, here's her web site http://www.freepowersong.com).

And because I'd actually like you to read through the Acknowledgements completely, I will lump everyone else here. My truly wonderful family (Mama-San, Marian and Carol) have been supportive 100%, always egging me on to get this thing published so they could read it. My friends would continually ask how it was going and I really didn't want to tell them that things sucked, so I kept at it and could then tell them things were moving ahead, albeit in a somewhat herky-jerky way (isn't that how writing books works?).

Finally, because this is where the rubber meets the road, Lindsay Marder has been an editor who hung in there with me. This can't be an easy job when the author needs to be educated in the entire process of producing a book. Who knew! Thanks, Lindsay, for holding my hand the whole way.

Okay, finally final are you, the Readers, because I'm hoping you gain something from reading this book…maybe even the willingness to follow your dream.

A PIRATE LOOKS AT 40...50...60...

INTRODUCTION

Ah, the good life…sitting in the shade of a palm tree on a white sand beach, cold drink in one hand, good book in the other.

Is that how you imagine a life abroad?

Maybe you envision rainforest adventures, with zip lining and horseback riding. If you are more continental-minded, a morning coffee on the piazza followed by an afternoon at an art museum may be more your style. Some adventurous types are more interested in exotic locations where the air is rich with incense and spices, and so is the food.

For people who have the urge to explore, retiring abroad can be an enticing prospect. There are many locations that offer adventure, luxurious surroundings, excellent real estate, and a low cost of living. The prospect of making those retirement dollars go further and providing you a better lifestyle is very alluring. That is especially true now, as economic challenges offer dwindling retirement accounts.

The world is full of expatriates (aka expats) looking for a rich lifestyle on a retirement budget. So they make that leap. After all, wouldn't they be crazy not to?

It says so right on the brochure.

But what happens next?

They find their perfect little place on the beach or apartment on the plaza. They're feeling pretty good about things in their new digs…until the electricity becomes spotty. The access to their computer and the Internet is cut off for several hours. They try to contact the electric company, but their high school Spanish doesn't cover those words and the utility worker who answers the phone does not understand.

Later, they get the electric bill and realize that the cost of living isn't as low as they'd been told. They start looking at their monetary plan and realize that they won't really be able to live the lifestyle they'd hoped.

Worse, they've been in their new country six months and haven't found any like-minded friends. They live in a beautiful city, in the home of their dreams with wonderful restaurants, and exciting amenities, but they've never felt more alone.

That is when paradise can feel like a nightmare.

Fortunately, you can avoid these types of discouraging scenarios by balancing the spontaneity of moving abroad with the preparation that a move like this requires. After all, as the saying goes: luck favors the prepared.

I should know. Like many retirees, I longed for my perfect retirement abroad. In the process of researching locations, I had my doubts and I had some roadblocks that were keeping me from making the leap. I researched countries in South and Central America. I went to International Living and Live & Invest Overseas conferences. I narrowed my choices down to the lovely city of Cuenca in Ecuador.

I was all set to move, when I realized that, while the location might be ideal for my dreams, there were other factors to consider. My family responsibilities made it nearly impossible for me to be in a place that was so far away. I had an aging dog, who couldn't fly, and a 93-year-old mother, who I wanted to be able to get back to quickly in an emergency. The move to Cuenca wasn't going to work for me just yet.

If I had jumped into that location before I was really ready, my perfect retirement dream would have been far from perfect. But with a little planning, I was able to find a location that was right for me now—one that would prepare me for my life in Ecuador later. This location put me in a better position to be able to take care of my family.

I could only make that decision because I had taken time to organize my true priorities. While I loved everything about Cuenca, I loved my family more.

Knowing your motivations, priorities, dreams, and aspirations can provide valuable clues to choosing the right location for you. It will also help you to determine what kind of life you want to live when you get there. Most importantly, it will help you avoid the syndrome of "the grass is always greener"—the belief that a glamorous new country will be the solution to whatever is going on in your life. You may logically know that a new country won't solve everything and yet your heart may still whisper that siren call.

So, how do you create a successful plan for retiring abroad? One that takes into account all the different issues that factor into such a move?

Sometimes, the hardest part about moving abroad is your own conflicting needs and desires. Maybe you want some place exotic, like Bali, but you need to be able to quickly get home to relatives. You might also want to live someplace that feels European, but has a third world cost of living. It is our conflicting desires that often trip us up when looking at locations. The good news is that there are so many wonderful places that could meet those needs, ones that aren't hyped by real estate companies or on the tourist routes. They just take a bit more patience and research to find.

The Happy Expat: Your Guide to Joyfully Retiring Abroad addresses several areas of consideration when retiring abroad:

» Prioritizing your basic needs

» Finding a location that fits your style of living

» Understanding the real cultural issues you'll be facing

» Readying yourself for change

» Overcoming any roadblocks and emotional pitfalls that get in your way

We'll address the reasons why some people never finish the journey of becoming expats. We'll also go over the complex issues that lead to so many expats returning back home in under two years. We'll cover those issues that can make an expat unsuccessful and give you solutions that you can put together before you even leave your home country.

You'll learn things like:

» What to do if (and when) you get homesick

» How to deal with emergencies

» What to do if you don't know the language

» How to budget for your new life

» How to handle change and unexpected conflicts with humor and fortitude

» What to do when exotic cultural adaptation becomes a headache

» How to maintain regular communication with those loved ones back home

» How to find other expats who speak your language and can act as guides and friends in your new life

All these issues are simple things that are often overlooked in the thrill of adventure. Being able to plan and organize your own solutions to these potentially challenging areas will put you ahead of the game and on track to a positive experience. You'll make decisions based on what's right for you, instead of being lured in by guidebook hype or special real estate deals.

So grab your favorite beverage, find a comfy spot, and begin the discovery that can lead to one of life's greatest adventures—living in a foreign land.

THAT'S WHAT LIVING IS TO ME

CHAPTER ONE: PRIORITIES

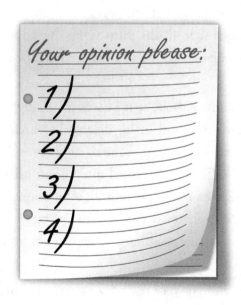

Have you ever daydreamed of your perfect life? The perfect place to live? How about a retirement that presents you with the time and money to do the things you love?

I certainly did. And because my passion is scuba diving, I thought about places like a Caribbean island or maybe Palau in Micronesia or even the coast of Australia.

I was juiced on the possibility of walking out my door and into the ocean every day if I wanted.

Then I sat down and really thought about it. I came to the surprising realization that, actually, I didn't want sand in my house or to have everything metal rust from the salty air to the point that it had to be replaced on a regular basis. And, truth be told, I didn't even want the beach lifestyle.

That was a complete shock to me because I thought that would be the lifestyle connecting me to my diving dream. I realized that what I wanted was access to dive whenever I wanted. However, I wanted my daily life to look very different. I wanted more of an urban and continental atmosphere. I wanted to be able to walk to boutique shops and hangout at cafes on a town square. I didn't want spring break bar crowds and grungy beachcombers as neighbors. I wanted sophisticated intellectuals for friendships and socializing.

So I sat back and got very real with myself. If I had focused on only one of my dreams (scuba diving) without taking into account any of my other dreams or my daily needs, I'd have chosen the wrong location. It would have been fun for about six months. After that, I'd have been lonely and frustrated.

I realized that I needed to get clear on what it was I really and truly wanted out of my adventure of retiring and living abroad.

And why I wanted it.

These are very important questions to ask before you make any moves. Otherwise, you can end up someplace that doesn't really give you what you're looking for; then, you may decide the whole living abroad thing was a huge mistake!

And no one wants that!

So let's start with a simple question—what are the five most important things you want in life? We are talking about things that, if you already had them in your life, would make you feel completely contented.

Do you know them?

Well, if you don't, don't feel badly. Most people don't. Our lives are so busy with just doing the day-to-day. We don't think maybe there's a better way.

The thing is, if you know what's most important to you, you can use that knowledge to make better choices, especially about choosing a location abroad.

So, how do you do that?

First, let's look at a few ideas to get your brain thinking in that direction.

Here are a few categories of desire (doesn't that sound like fun?) that have a powerful influence over the happiness levels of your life:

1. Who are the people who must remain in your "in group" and what type of people would you like to add to that group when living abroad?

2. What are the things you need to do regularly to stay grounded and happy? (Example: exercise, philanthropy, travel, church)

3. What are your goals and dreams? (Example: maintain dependable income, help educate impoverished children, learn to make wine)

Make a "Big List" of everything you think would make your life complete. This is a list of your Life Priorities. This is not a list of daily needs such as having a washer and dryer in your house, unless that is something you cannot and will not negotiate because life as you know it will end and it takes precedence over just about everything else you can possibly imagine. (Those things will come in a later exercise.)

List a minimum of fifteen things—and keep each "thing" simple. Why? Because the more complicated you make each Life Priority, the more difficult it will be to attain.

For example, write "I continue to travel the globe" instead of "every year I take two 1 month vacations that include scuba diving, plus a trip back home to visit friends and family, and I also take a cultural trip to Europe..." You get what I'm talking about. Keep it simple.

Step 1: Write your "Big List" of Life Priorities here as if each one is already a done deal (e.g., Using the present tense: I am, I have, etc. not I will have, I will be):

_____

_____

_____

_____

_____

_____

_____

_____

_____

_____

_____

_____

_____

_____

_____

_____

_____

_____

_____

_____

_____

Now take a look at your list. Are there certain ones that stand out as "must have's?" Mark the list above in order of importance from one to ten. Even if you have twenty items on the list, you are only going to mark the top ten.

Got them? Good!

Step 2: List those ten here in order of importance and continue to use the present tense:

_____

_____

_____

_____

_____

_____

_____

_____

_____

_____

_____

_____

_____

_____

_____

_____

_____

_____

_____

_____

Now, I'd like you to take a look and see if one of your Top Ten is about travel, moving, or living overseas? If it isn't, that's okay. You may be looking to move abroad because it will help you attain one or more of the items on your Top Ten list. Is that true? If so, you are set with your Top Ten.

If it isn't true, then, it is critical to your success that you figure out why you want to move overseas. Give this some serious thought, jot down ideas, test them for importance, and then write down clearly why you want to move abroad.

_____

Once you've done that, pick the least important of your Top Ten and replace it with the 'why' you identified, written in the present tense. For example, "I am stretching my retirement dollars so I can travel more" or "I teach English as a foreign language."

If one of your Top Ten is about living or traveling abroad or if doing so will help you achieve one of your Top Ten, then you know you are definitely headed in the right direction.

Now I'm going to ask you to do something strange—*If the words moving/living abroad are on your list, then temporarily take that item off and replace it with something else from your Big List.* The reason behind this action is so you can really focus on your what's most important to you *within your life abroad.* So, for this exercise, living abroad is a given.

Imagine if, during your lifetime, you were only allowed to have the top five of your Top Ten list. Would that make a difference in your order? Compare each of your top five with the remaining five. Does the order need to be changed? You may find yourself swapping out which ones are in the top five. It is always interesting to see what becomes most important if you can only have the top five. [Don't panic—choosing five doesn't mean you can't, ultimately, have it all. This exercise is just to focus you on those critical must haves, without the distraction of all the others.]

Step 3: When you have finished reviewing your Top Ten and decided on which are the most important to you, list your Top Five Life Priorities below:

_____

_____

_____

_____

_____

_____

_____

_____

_____

_____

_____

_____

_____

_____

_____

_____

_____

_____

Congratulations! You are now ahead of most people in the world. You know exactly what is most important to you.

At this point you may be asking why you went through that exercise. Was it just a feel good exercise?

No way!

Ultimately, your **Top Five Life Priorities are critical** to selecting your **perfect location abroad!**

Why? Because, if your new location abroad doesn't feed those needs, then you will end up unhappy.

However, there are a few steps you need to take before you can use these Life Priorities to choose a new location. Let's start with how each of those Top Five can be incorporated into a move abroad.

Here's an example of a how I incorporated my Life Priorities into my move.

Ann's Initial Top Five:

» I enjoy a terrific relationship with my ideal partner

» I continue to travel the globe

» I live each day with clarity of passion

» I work with a team that takes care of the details of my life

» I help others improve their lives

As you can see, this list has a variety of interests. It's important to figure out a way of incorporating your interests into your move abroad. Here's an example of how it's done:

Top 5 Life Priorities	How can I achieve this while living abroad?	What are my other options?
I enjoy a terrific relationship with my ideal partner.	I want this person in my life before I move.	I will search for a partner here and let him know my passion for living abroad. My ideal partner will need to share this passion and be able to go with me.
I continue traveling the globe	My options for travel will be limited if I buy a place abroad. I will rent places and stay in a country for several months, then move to a different country.	I could settle down in one country permanently that is close to other countries I want to visit. Or I could choose to travel frequently but not fully move abroad.
I work with a team that takes care of the details of my life.	I set up people in the U.S. to help with my business. We communicate via Internet. I also live in a place where I can hire help to take care of my household needs.	I may need to find an employee who can travel with me.

Now it's time for you to evaluate your own list:

Top 5 Life Priorities	How can I achieve this while living abroad?	What are my other options?

Great! Now you have put together a plan that will allow you to express your true passions while living abroad.

At this point you are probably thinking *yeah, yeah, yeah, that's all fine and dandy, but what about the day-to-day stuff? Living in another country can be so different than the way I'm used to living. Don't I need to consider that, too?*

Funny you should ask. That's actually the next step.

Sometimes it's the simplest daily activities that can trip us up. I think of my friend Mary who is a coffee connoisseur. If she ended up living where she couldn't find good coffee beans, she would think she'd fallen into a living Hell. This might not be one of her top Life Priorities, but it sure would make a difference in her day-to-day happiness quotient.

So, let's look at what your daily needs are.

To get you in the mood, here's a true story I heard about some expats in Cuenca, Ecuador (names have been changed, as they say, to protect the innocent). This experience might spark some thoughts about what's important to you on a daily basis.

Mike and Dee, along with a couple of their friends, Pete and Carol, went hiking in the Cajas Mountains near Cuenca. They were heading home, just finishing the last leg of the hike down when Mike stepped, twisted his ankle, and fell. End result—one broken leg. So now what? Pete and Carol finished the hike so that they could use their cell phone to call Mike's doctor and find out what to do. Mike's doctor told them that the best orthopedic surgeon in Ecuador happened to be associated with their clinic right in Cuenca and that's where they should take Mike.

So Pete and Carol found a door (that had to be a story in itself) and hauled it up the mountain, with a little help from the new friends they made in the process. Mike was loaded onto the door, carried down the last part of the mountain, positioned into their vehicle, and driven to his doctor's clinic. From there, Mike was examined, x-rayed, the leg was set, he was given meds, and instructions on what to do. After all that, Mike and Dee went home after paying their bill. And the bill? Just under $1,500 for everything, including the orthopedic specialist.

Why tell this story? Because it might trigger some ideas about what's important for your day-to-day list. Sometimes we forget about those items we take for granted back in our own countries. Are items like low cost healthcare or an ambulance service important to you? What about other areas of infrastructure like access to clean water or international calls? Most countries have infrastructure in place, but the quality may be different to what you are used to having. When thinking about daily living, those necessities and infrastructure issues are important.

And now you get to use the same process you used before to identify your top daily needs. Remember, you're doing this so you can make intelligent and informed decisions about where you want to live.

To get you jump-started on creating your list of Daily Top Five, here is a list of possibilities:

- Lots of restaurant choices
- Running water - indoors!
- Well-stocked grocery stores
- Modern shopping mall
- Unique craft stores
- Good language schools
- Shops offering the latest fashions (or whatever is important to you)
- Basic housing (define what that means to you)
- Easy access to an international airport
- Good public transportation
- Reliable cell phone reception
- Temperatures in the 70s and 80s year round
- Pet-friendly
- Able to walk most places I want to go
- Easy access to practitioners of alternative medicine (homeopathic, alternative, chiropractic, shaman, etc.)
- Good roads that don't require 4WD
- Clean drinking water out of the tap

- Low crime rate (what is your definition of crime)
- Active expat community
- Able to return to US home in 8-10 hours
- Reliable broadband service
- Safe beaches within walking distance
- Inexpensive household help
- Low to moderate humidity
- Lots of cultural events and opportunities
- Low cost of living (what is your definition)
- Residency requirements easy to meet
- Solid infrastructure (electricity, phone, etc.)
- Employment opportunities
- Variety of ethnic foods
- English speaking doctors
- Luxury housing (define what that means to you)
- Shops with the latest technology
- Movies in English
- House with a yard (be clear on what 'yard' means to you)

Look over the lists above to get some ideas. Then make your own list below. Write down a minimum of fifteen.

Step 1: Your Daily Priority "Big List":

_____

_____

_____

_____

_____

_____

_____

_____

_____

_____

_____

_____

_____

_____

_____

_____

_____

Now, you'll do exactly the same process as you did with your Top Life Priorities. Take a look at your list. Are there certain ones that stand out as "must have's?" Mark the list above in order of importance from one to ten. Even if you have twenty items on the list, you are only going to mark the top ten.

Got them? Good!

Step 2: List those ten here in order of importance:

_____

_____

_____

_____

_____

_____

_____

_____

_____

_____

What I'd like you to do now is to look over your list from Step 2. Ask yourself, if you could only have five of those items in your new location, what would they be? Compare them one to another until you know your Top Five Daily Priorities and write them below.

Step 3: Your Top Five Daily Priorities

_____

_____

_____

_____

_____

_____

_____

_____

Look over this list. Read it out loud. Does it feel right to you—are these your most important daily priorities? Are there any priorities from your "Big List" that you need to rethink or replace in the top five? Make any adjustments you need to until it feels right. Since you'll be using these five to help you make decisions about the right location for you, it's important you take the time to be sure.

Now that you have both your Top Five Life Priorities and your Top Five Daily Priorities, it's time to check out how they mesh with each other.

Complete the Side-By-Side Chart below by filling in each column from the two lists you've completed.

Side-By-Side Chart	
Top Five Life Priorities	*Top Five Daily Priorities*

Look over both lists. Would the items on these lists create your ideal living situation? Is anything of importance missing that you need to add? If so, add it here:

_____

_____

_____

_____

_____

Comparing lists, are there any conflicts between the lists? If there are conflicts between your wants and your needs, use this space to work out the details of how to make them compatible or if you need to re-evaluate some part of your plan:

_____

_____

_____

_____

_____

_____

_____

_____

_____

_____

_____

_____

_____

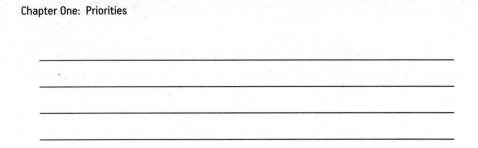

Be sure to update the Side-By-Side Chart above if you have made any changes in either your Top Five Life Priorities or Top Five Daily Priorities.

As I said before, you are so far ahead of where most people are who are thinking about moving abroad. You know exactly what you want in your new life and can make intelligent and informed decisions.

Be ready to reap the joy and just downright have fun from living in a place that "fits" you.

THE WANDERER

CHAPTER TWO: OPTIONS FOR RETIRING ABROAD

Before we get too far into a book about living abroad, it's important to toss out there that settling down in another country may not be the right option for you. You may like the idea of an adventure abroad, but don't feel ready for a full time commitment. Or maybe you see yourself as more of a world traveler who doesn't want to settle down in a particular country.

A retirement abroad can be as creative as you want it to be. There are many expats who have taken creative approaches to living their "overseas adventure".

Which brings me to a quick review of what, exactly, the word "expat", as used in this book, actually means.

Being an expat means not living in the country where you were born. It does not mean giving up citizenship. It does not mean you don't love your home country. It only means you are living elsewhere for any number of reasons for some period of time and that timeframe can range from a few months a year to the rest of your life.

Now that we have that out of the way, let's take a look at the many ways that expats are living their lives. Maybe one of their strategies will work for you!

» Full Time

» Part Time, Temporary, or Snow-birding

» Base Camp

» Vagabonding

» Cruising

Full Time

Living abroad full time is exactly what you think it is. There are many who choose this approach because they enjoy having their home in one place. For example, these are the folks who, when you ask where they live, will tell you "Cuenca, Ecuador". They don't go on to say, "well, actually, only part time" or "I don't really spend a lot of time there as I do a lot of traveling". They tell you their home is Cuenca, Ecuador because that's where they spend most, if not all, of their time.

Full time means this is where you wash your clothes, create a community for yourself, and open bank accounts. It's the place where you invite family and friends to visit so they can share your enthusiasm for your new life. This is also where you have discovered the hidden pastry shop, found the farmer who raises organically fed chickens, and it's where you return after any excursion out of that location.

It's home, all the time, every day of the year.

But how do you do it?

Very carefully.

When you want to move abroad full time, it's important to choose wisely. Regardless of where you go, there is a financial cost, as well as the emotional cost, and both need to be considered. Chapter 7 gets into a lot of detail about how to choose a location and is based on the work you did in Chapter 1.

Budget

Unlike the other options, full time budget planning is just like what you would do if you remain where you are now. You aren't trying to budget for more than one place to live and, other than any ongoing expenses back in your home country, your budget will look pretty much like the one you have now. Except, of course, your money will most likely go much further.

Living Conditions

When living abroad full time, you will be living in a house or apartment in a city, town, village, or countryside where you will spend most of your time. Make sure it provides you the life you want to live. Use the work you did in Chapter 1 and the work you'll do in Chapter 6 to help you make your decisions.

One important aspect of your decision-making will be what you bring with you. Chapter 9 goes into this in more detail. However, be sure that you include a few items that, when you unpack them, will make you feel that "this is home". I cannot stress how important it is for you to be able to look around and feel that your new home is familiar.

Benefits & Drawbacks of Full Time

Benefits:

» Learn the in's and out's of only one new place

» Budgeting is more straightforward

» Really become part of the community

» One and done

Drawbacks:

» Possibly burning bridges and then changing your mind

» Homesickness might become overwhelming

» Depending on distance, it can be very expensive to visit family and friends

Snowbird, Part Time and/or Temporary

For those who have obligations back home—whether it be business, family, or community—that prevent them from moving abroad full time, there is the option of living abroad part time. Part time could mean month long trips, several times a year. It could mean staying for three to six months. And for some, it might be that you just want someplace to get away from the cold winters.

The temporary option is for those folks who are not yet sure where their perfect place is located. They prefer to stay in a specific location for a relatively short period of time to try it out. Then they return home to evaluate the experience. The next time, they choose a different location. For them, it's repeat until they find that location they consider **the** one place for them.

For example, I have always been intrigued with the idea of living in Paris, so I decided that would be a place I'd try out. My boyfriend was game to try it as well, so we rented a very small apartment on the Left Bank. During the time we were there, we lived "locally", meaning we used the shops that were nearby for all our food and beverage needs, ate in the small cafes, sought out expats to learn more about living there, did the laundry in the local laundromat (pulling our wheeled suitcase along the street as the easiest way to carry the laundry), and used local transportation to get around.

Then it was time to evaluate whether to extend our time or reconsider. As much as we loved Paris, we realized that it wasn't in the cards for us at that time and returned to the U.S.

Next up was Baja, Mexico. I was going to be on my own, since my boyfriend needed to remain in Colorado for at least another year for his work.

I went to Rosarito, Baja California, Mexico on a temporary basis to check it out. I spent a month to find out whether or not I wanted to stay longer. Before the end of the month, I was already sure I wanted to spend an additional several months. So I got busy finding a place that would suit me for a longer period of time. And I also needed to find a place that would be less expensive.

What I learned while I was in the one month trial was that paying month-to-month was the most expensive way to go (no surprise there). It also wasn't much less expensive to rent for four to five months. The first time there was any real difference was at the six-month mark. Fortunately, I was ready for six more months as my next trial period and was able to save $200 per month. If I'd had more time to shop around, I could probably have saved an additional $100-$200 per month. However, since I hadn't given myself enough time, I had to settle for what I could find quickly. Trust me, four weeks is too short a time to test a place out, then decide to stay longer, and then find a real deal on rent. I had given myself only ten days to find my next place. It was a little crazy during that time, but I lived through it. Whew!

Live and learn.

Then I was on to my next step—the six-month trial period. During that six months, when I was considering whether or not I'd actually want to spend an even longer time in Mexico, I was looking for the necessary infrastructure that I preferred (things like broadband, dependable utilities, convenient grocery shopping, etc.), plus the social connections that would make it fun for a year. I wanted friendships, a strong expat community, and I realized this part of Mexico was a place I'd enjoy spending a lot of time.

There are so many variations on this theme of part-time, temporary and snow birding. For some people, they mix it up a bit.

One option is that if you are in the early stages of planning a retirement abroad, maybe you decide on two to four trips over the next couple years or so, for a few weeks each time, just to try out some different locations. Then, once you've decided on a place that really feels right to you, you plan a longer stay to try it out. You still haven't made a commitment and can change your mind if the longer stay raises some concerns that you didn't have previously with the shorter visit.

Another option is for the many people who become "traveling snowbirds," heading to tropical locations during the winter and returning home during the summer months. This gives them a feel for each location so that they can narrow their choices down to the ones they truly want.

But how do you do it?

For many people, these are great options. But short-term trips require a lot of planning. You'll want to consider the following:

» Budget
» Living conditions
» "Trying on" the location
» Developing relationships

Budget

The most important consideration when trying a part time or temporary style of retirement abroad is your budget. This style can be costly if you aren't careful. Renting a place for a few weeks or a few months will be much more expensive than renting for six months or a year. Be sure to put together an annual budget for what you want to spend. Then do your research on the location. Are there cheaper places that are not right on the beach or in the center of town?

You may want to downsize your life at home so you can afford to take more trips. It is a great way to prepare yourself for an ultimate move abroad.

This is another personal decision. The methods of downsizing to make room for your travel budget are similar to those that you would consider if you weren't leaving at all.

» Selling your home
» Temporarily taking on a tenant
» Selling your home to rent a smaller apartment or home
» Renting out your home while you're away

Many people also don't consider the little habits they can scale back on. Consider cutting out:

» Movie tickets (sign up for Netflix or Hulu Plus for the price of one movie in a theater)

» Book shopping (become an active library user)

» Coffee (cut back on outside purchases, buy good beans & become your own barista)

» Smoking (stop if that's in the cards for you, cut down if it isn't)

» Eating out (cut back to once a week or whatever works for you. Pick one night each week to treat yourself to a really great meal at home, complete with your favorite beverage and a yummy dessert)

Living conditions

Since you are only going to be in your trial location for a short time, you won't be bringing furniture and lots of comfort items. In the nicest way I know to suggest it: suck it up! You won't want to cart around tons of suitcases and spend the money shipping furniture for a temporary period of time. That means renting a furnished home or apartment. If you plan to stay for a month or more, you may want to choose a comfortably furnished place over the ones that are more fashionable or closest to the beach or other attractions. You'll want to feel like you are living there, not just visiting. Do bring a few comfort items – photographs, your favorite pillow, certain sheets if you prefer them, and your own linens. Hauling large items is what we're avoiding here. If you aren't willing to compromise, don't even consider moving abroad. Flexibility is a must.

Also, check with the owner or real estate agent before you rent, to find out how stocked the kitchen is and inquire about the condition of the bathroom towels and sheets. They should be able to send you a list of the home's appliances, cookware and silverware. Keep in mind that what you consider to be the bare essentials may be considered extravagant where you are considering staying. So even when it sounds like everything is covered, be prepared for some surprises. For example, I wanted sharp kitchen knives and the first place I stayed in Baja had what I considered to be subpar kitchen knives. So I bought a set of cooking knives at Costco, each with its own cover and in all different colors. Now I just take them with me. They are easy to pack and weigh very little...and they are sharp.

Trying On The Location - Not Vacationing

If you are going to try one or both of these approaches, remember that you are not doing this for a vacation. It's great to have fun and see the sights, but remember to try to live like a local as much as you can. If you decide it's the right place, you can do the sightseeing when you live there.

If not, you can always go back for a real vacation!

Developing Relationships

While you are in these locations, this is a great time to explore the local expat community. Get to know some people. Go to events. Find out where everyone hangs out. See if they offer clubs, activities, and sports that you like to do. Get a feel for the lifestyle. If your trip ends and you find that you have treasured friendships, then this might be the place for you. However, if you feel uncomfortable or the lifestyle doesn't match your needs, then you know you can cross that location off the list as a potential retirement spot.

You may be wondering about whether it makes sense to take a short trip of, say, four weeks and spend time and energy connecting with the expat community when you aren't sure you'd want to stay. Maybe you think you should spend your time staying in a couple of different locations in the same country, or take side trips to get a feel of where you might travel, when you want a short break from living in that location.

The answer is that you really want to try out one place for the full four weeks. Do your homework while you're still in the U.S., Canada, or wherever you call home. Know enough about the location that you'll know what's nearby.

Your time truly needs to be spent living like a local, and that includes connecting with the expat community. That is one of the most important connections you can make. Why? Because they can answer so many of your questions, make suggestions on where to eat, buy groceries, go for entertainment, and a myriad of other bits of information that you will use to decide if this is the place where you want to spend more time. And in the process of making these connections, you'll discover if there are folks living there whose company you would enjoy.

When I spent six weeks in Cuenca, Ecuador, I did exactly what I'm suggesting you do. And I met some wonderful people with whom I am still in touch. I found out that Cuenca is a place I could easily call home...except that it's too far for me right now. So it's a place I go for vacation to hang with my friends and enjoy the wonderfulness of Cuenca. Can you tell how much I love this place?

Benefits & Drawbacks of Snowbird, Part Time and/or Temporary

Benefits:

» Can help you try out potential retirement locations.

» Ease your friends and family into the idea of you ultimately moving abroad.

» A way to have your cake and eat it too (adventure abroad and life at home).

» A great way to get a reluctant spouse to try the idea out and see if it will work.

Drawbacks:

» Cost

» Getting enough time off to make the trip valuable.

» The tendency to want to vacation, instead of live as a local.

Base Camp

Maybe for you, retirement is a time for adventuring. One the most affordable ways to do that is to find a place where you can create an inexpensive base camp. All you need to do is choose a location that is surrounded by many areas you would like to explore

How do you do it?

The first thing you do is pick a region whose secrets you'd like to uncover. Decide on a time period for living and traveling in that area. It could be six months, a year, or maybe even five. Then search out cities and towns within that region that are inexpensive, comfortable, and safe. Make sure it is somewhat centrally located to the areas where you'd like to explore. Rent a place and find a low cost vehicle or familiarize yourself with the public transportation.

Budgeting

As previously discussed, if you are renting for a year or more, you can get good rates on rent. However, it's important for you to decide where your priorities are. If your priority is to travel a region and have adventures, then that is where your budget needs to be focused. That means maybe you won't be putting a big chunk of your budget toward a large place or one that is in a prime location. Instead, find someplace that is close to a bunch of great travel destinations, but far enough away that it doesn't have the high cost of living.

What you'll spend the bulk of your money on will be lodging and other travel expenses for your trips. You may want to start with day trips where you can come back home and avoid spending too much right away. Consider it putting your toe in the water, rather than diving in fully clothed. If you are in Europe, you can save money by looking for pensions or hostels, instead of hotels. Some areas of Latin America have hostels, but the hotels in many Latin countries are very affordable.

Living Conditions

Your living conditions can depend on how much travel you want to do. Who needs a big house when you are going to spend most of your days away from it? Do you want to live in Paris, but decide on a tiny apartment in a less trendy neighborhood? Do you want to live in a lovely cottage in the Czech Republic and explore the surrounding countryside? Maybe you'd like to live on the island of Ambergris Caye in Belize and spend time exploring the islands and the coast of Central America?

This is another situation where you are going to need to rent furnished apartments or homes. Make sure you follow the same instructions we gave in the Snowbird, Part time, and Temporary section. Get a list of the appliances, linens, household furnishings, and kitchen utensils. Make sure the space is something you can live with, even if it isn't in an upscale location. Leasing agents and owners will send you pictures, but they will obviously be the best pictures they have. This is another reason to develop relationships with expats. Explain to them where you're looking to rent, include the link, and ask if they have an opinion on it.

Since you probably won't be flying over to check the place out before you sign a contract, Google Maps can be an asset in your search. They have street views of many cities and towns. Drive around the neighborhood of the place you are considering by using Google's street view before you sign a lease or put any deposits down.

Benefits & Drawbacks of a Base Camp

Benefits:

» You can live and travel through some of the world's top destinations.

» When you stay for at least a year in a location, you get the benefit of cheaper rent.

» It's a great way to sample a region to see if there's anywhere you'd like to settle after you are finished traveling.

» You'll have more home time than pure travel would give you. This allows you to make friends and build relationships with people.

» Your family and friends have one place where they can reach you or send you a card.

Drawbacks:

» May not be able to be in the best locations or nicest homes.

» May not offer as much travel as you may want.

» You may be liable to treat it more as a vacation, instead of creating relationships.

Vagabonding

What if you don't want to live in just one place? Maybe you want to see the world during your retirement. That's what vagabonding is all about. People get very creative with their budget and their time so that they can keep moving from country to country, seeing and experiencing the entire world.

Sound like a lot of work? It can be. It definitely takes planning and you must be comfortable with living out of a few suitcases. But there are retired folks who are living their dream by traveling the world. Most of these sorts of trips will be months long and an in-depth exploration of the area.

I met one couple that have been vagabonding for years all over Asia. What they do is set themselves up in a place, perhaps Thailand, and stay there for one to two years. By the time they move on, they have made some terrific friends, explored dozens of places in Thailand, and best of all, taken enough trips to other areas that they know where they want to go next, like Hanoi. And then do it all over again. Then pick Malaysia for their next trip. And they just keep moving on.

Eventually, they will do what other friends of mine have done. After exploring all around Asia, they picked where they wanted to live and settled there. They still travel and now it's all about vacations!

How do you do it?

Like I said earlier, this style of retirement takes a lot of planning. Whole books can be written on the possibilities. I won't be able to go over a lot of detail here, but I can get you started thinking about the possibilities.

Write down a list of all your dream destinations. Don't leave any out, even if they seem over your budget. The key is to be creative. It's amazing the deals you can find with a bit of research.

Since budgeting is so much a part of how this style of retirement is accomplished, let's go straight into...

Budget

First, you will need to determine an annual budget. If you have a financial planner, talk it over with him or her. If you don't, take on that role for yourself. Look at whether you will need to downsize your life to accomplish the goal. Do you still need that big house or could selling it help you to realize your dreams?

Once you have your budget, start looking at all the places you put on your list that you want to visit. Investigate the cost of living in each of those places. Determine the travel costs to get there.

Now it's time to start fitting locations into your budget. Maybe you'll start by spending most of the year exploring less expensive locations in Asia, Africa, or South America. You may even find that sometimes travel in those regions can be cheaper than your expenses at home. And if your budget allows, treat yourself and splurge on four to six weeks in Sydney, Paris, or Hong Kong.

You could even throw in some couch surfing if that works for you. If you're not familiar with the concept, here's a link where you can check it out (Couchsurfing.org). Be very careful if you chose to go this route from time-to-time. You'll be staying in someone's house, someone you don't actually know, so you want to pay close attention to any feedback and/ or recommendations from others who have stayed there. Ask questions about anything you don't understand or that concerns you. And if you feel there is a red flag, trust your instinct.

As you can see, I'm hesitant about couch surfing. However, that's a personal thing for me. You should also know that I met a retired nurse who has had very good experiences with couch surfing. I met her through a physician friend of mine who has couch surfed in many countries and met wonderful people who have made his visit to their locations truly positive experiences. And he also suggests that people use common sense when choosing a host.

Another way to vagabond is to toss in some of the Base Camping approach to lower your rental costs. Maybe rent for six months to explore a region, before moving on to another part of the world.

Benefits & Drawbacks

Benefits:

» You can see the world's top destinations.

» Never get bored with a location. Life would always be an adventure.

» A great way to sample the world to see if there's anywhere you'd like to settle after you are finished traveling.

» Experience many interesting cultures, foods, and lifestyles.

Drawbacks:

» May not be able to be in the best locations or nicest homes.

» May get tired of traveling and living out of a suitcase.

» Very difficult to create lasting relationships. It can get lonely.

» Not as easy to stay connected with people back home.

» May be expensive without a lot of planning and research.

» You'd need to research the healthcare aspects of the places you will be traveling.

Cruising

For some people, travel isn't enough. You may want to actually define the type of travel. Maybe you want to see the world by ship. That may mean having a permanent cabin on a specific cruise line or it may be that you take the voyage on a yacht or sailing ship.

How do you do it?

Yachting

If you are considering buying your own yacht, then you have a lot of work to prepare for that type of retirement. You will need to be very educated in the sailing, maintenance, and upkeep of a ship. Yachting, in this way, takes a special kind of crazy passion. You can't just love travel; you have to love the whole experience of having a yacht. It will mean close quarter living, not much bathroom space, lots of work and upkeep on the ship, and an eye for weather.

If this sounds like the life for you, I recommend checking out this website: http://www.billdietrich.me/GettingStarted.html

It is the diary of a man who decided that the sailing life was for him. He's outlined many of the thought processes and considerations he had to go through in finding a boat, deciding what type of sailing he wanted to do, and included many recommendations from people who had already done it.

Cruising

If you are more about luxury travel by sea and less about the experience of owning and maintaining a boat, then cruising is a better option for you. There are several options for a cruise retirement:

Traditional Cruises

With the traditional cruises you have the choice of staying on the same 7 to 14 day itinerary and doing it over and over, or you can hop from ship to ship, with different destinations.

Long Cruises

Long cruises can be more affordable and range from 20 days to 115 days.

Yacht Cruises

Sharing a yacht with the owner for a month, a quarter of a year, or more. You help pay for the upkeep, but they do the work and often they have a staff who will provide you with all your meals.

Buying a Cabin on a Ship

With the increased popularity of cruise retirements, a number of companies now offer cabins for sale in private cruise ships. These ships often consult with their owners about each year's itinerary. They also stay longer in each port, from a week to a month. You have all the amenities of a cruise ship, with the security of being an owner.

A very good friend of mine told me about meeting a 90-year-old man on a cruise she took in the Mediterranean. He was in reasonably good health, but needed someone to help him with many of his day-to-day needs. So he hired a nurse to travel with him. Every day she helped him prepare for the day, escorted him to breakfast, and then they headed on up to one of the decks with some protection from the elements and a killer view. He spent the day reading, napping, talking with other guests, and generally enjoyed himself. My friend spent time talking with him and he was pretty happy with his life and was very clear that it beat the hell out of living in a nursing home or assisted living!

Budget

Because this style of retirement covers a lot of ground, it is difficult to provide a lot of details regarding budget. This is not the most affordable form of retirement, but it can be one that gives you a lot of bang for your buck. With cruise rates dropping due to the economy and yachts becoming available for less than you'd pay for a small house, there are ways to make this work within a retirement budget.

The trick is to get smart about it. One couple I read about was able to lower their cruise costs by checking with cruise lines about when they moved their ships from dry dock to their point of embarkation for a six month itinerary. By booking on those reduced cost trips, they were able to relocate to other countries where they could then take local cruises for lower prices. By boarding in another country, they found many cruises were far more affordable than the U.S. rates for the same cruise. They even found that joining a cruise on the second or third day of the itinerary offered substantial discounts.

You will find that long cruises tend to be more affordable than the short cruises. You can find 100-115 day world cruises starting at $15,000-20,000 per person. Now before you choke on that number, remember it's for nearly half the year and you'll have all your food and other amenities included, plus you'll get to travel to interesting ports. And...you only unpack once!

If a seafaring retirement is your dream, your best bet is to define your annual budget, then do your research to find the situation that best meets your needs.

Benefits & Drawbacks

Benefits:

» You can see the world's top destinations.

» Never get bored with a location. Life would always be an adventure.

» A great way to sample the world to see if there's anywhere you'd like to settle after you are finished traveling.

» Be completely pampered (cruising) and never have to cook or do dishes.

Drawbacks:

» May not be within a particular budget.

» May get tired of traveling and living out of a suitcase.

» Very difficult to create lasting relationships. It can get lonely.

» Cruise ships can be noisy or overwhelming.

» Not as easy to stay connected with people back home.

» May be expensive without a lot of planning and research.

» Do you have the stomach for sea travels? Constant jostling can be take its toll.

As you can see, there are many options for an adventurous retirement.

It's just a matter of determining your wants and needs, matching them to your budget, and then planning, planning, planning!

MONEY, MONEY, MONEY

CHAPTER THREE:
AFFORDABILITY

Ah, money! Income. Budget. I love the first two but the last... not so much. Regardless of my opinions, I know that before I get all packed up to move, I need to make sure I can afford my new life abroad and have a plan for supporting that life. You will, too! Let's start with your reasons for moving.

People move abroad for many reasons. Some are retiring, others want a lower cost of living, and many are on an adventure or educational stay. You will want to evaluate your financial plans for living abroad. Are you looking to retire more affordably? Do you want to run a business or work in the country? Are you going for educational and cultural experiences? Write down your financial issues for living abroad here:

(psst.. all the work you did in Chapters 1 & 2 should make this a snap!)

_____

_____

_____

_____

_____

_____

_____

_____

_____

_____

_____

_____

_____

Knowing your purpose for living abroad means you will need to research laws and requirements that will affect your achievement of that purpose. Be sure to look up the regulations for your purpose, which may include some of the following:

» Working/earning an income as an employee

» Starting or running a business

» Hiring employees

» Owning or renting property

» Retirement benefits

» Banking requirements (Some countries allow you to hold U.S. currency in a local bank account, others do not.)

» The tax laws of your own country (The U.S. requires citizens to file tax returns, even when out of country, no exceptions.)

» Residency requirements (Some countries require fees or proof of outside income.)

After you learn about potential fees, taxes and costs of moving to your country of choice, you can put together a more accurate budget. Your budget will then need to consider all the normal costs of living. Things you will need to take into consideration:

» Are you on a fixed income/budget or will your income be flexible/variable?

» Do you want to rent or own property?

» Will you take your car, rent or buy a car there, or use bikes/public transportation?

» What types of utilities, Internet, cell phone or other services will you need? Are they available in the location of your choice?

» What sorts of amenities do you need?

Let's explore each of these options and how they will affect your budget while living abroad.

Fixed Income or Doing Business?

Fixed Income or Budget

If you are on a fixed income or a strict budget, you will need to pay particular attention to the cost of living in the area where you choose to live. Do as much research as you can before you leave. Get to know what the true costs of things will be and not just what a guide tells you. You may want to buy a small ledger or budgeting software to help you determine your true financial picture and build a budget that will work in your daily life. The topics brought up in the rest of this chapter will help you to create a more honest financial picture. (If you plan a 2-3 month trial visit to your new home, you will be able to gather a ton of information about the cost of living.)

Working or Owning a Business

If you plan to continue to work while overseas, your income may be more than those on a fixed income, but you are also subject to the whim of the economy and the challenges of doing business overseas. One important piece to include in your financial plan is to create and maintain a cushion of money that will tide you over should there be a change in your income stream.

Another area to pay attention to is how you handle your taxes. Be sure to find a tax person who is experienced in working with people who live abroad and continue to run their own business or are employed by someone else. Whoever you use now may be great for all your tax work in the States or wherever you reside. Just understand that living outside your home country and receiving income or running a business is an entirely different situation and you need someone doing your taxes who knows and understands how the tax laws will apply to you. Most tax folks only understand the laws that apply within their own country borders. So I highly encourage you to take the time to find someone who regularly works with expats. It will be beneficial to your financial health.

Additionally, you may want to build up a nest egg or cushion before you head to your new home. That way, if you experience a sudden drop in customers or you have a week without Internet service, you can feel confident that you will still be able to pay your expenses. It also would benefit you to put a percentage of your income into savings for the same reason.

Create a Cushion

Just as it is back home, knowing you can handle the unexpected makes for a much better night's sleep. You want to make sure you have enough wherewithal to take care of an emergency or drop in income. That cushion can be the difference between breathing easy and enjoying yourself and wondering every day if you'll be able to handle an unexpected outflow of cash.

So what are the things you should think about to know how much you need in your financial cushion?

» The cost of an emergency trip back to your home country, e.g., the US, Canada, etc.

» Enough money to cover 1-2 months of expenses in your new location

» Enough money to cover 1-2 months of expenses that still exist for you in your home country

» Enough money to cover an emergency surgery, hospital stay, and medications.

How much that is in actual dollars is part of what you need to figure out as you put together your budget.

Rent or Own?

Your biggest living expense will be housing. How large a chunk this takes out of your budget will depend on a number of factors:

» Where do you plan to live? European countries have a much higher cost of putting a roof over your head, similar to the United States and Canada. Second and third world nations will be much less expensive. However, deals can be found in any country and living outside the hub of a big city or tourist area can reduce your expenses considerably.

» What type of dwelling do you want? Obviously, a large home will be more expensive, both in upkeep and in rent or mortgage, than a small apartment. Sometimes it is easy to get carried away when we see something that catches our fancy. Put together your budget in advance. Know how much you have to spend each month and stick to your budget when it's time to rent or buy.

» How long do you plan to stay? If you only plan to stay in the country for a year or less, you will get more bang for your buck to rent. It will also cost you less in upkeep and save you the hassle of trying to sell or rent it after you leave. Do some research on the area where you want to live.

» What if the area where you want to live is beyond your budget? If so, what other options do you have? Are there less expensive neighborhoods nearby? Check the Internet for hidden gems. Find a local expat group and ask them about neighborhoods that might meet your requirements and your price range. Contact real estate agents for the area.

» What are the reasons for buying, instead of renting? If you plan to buy a place, be very clear about your reasons. Do you want to live there for an extended period of time? Is it in a location that has a high demand for rentals if you decide to only live there part time, or not at all? What is the housing market like in that area? Do homes sell quickly? Does the market fluctuate dramatically? Are the buyers local or does it depend on a foreign market that can drastically affect values in a down economy? Think through your reasons and your ability to sell when and if you decide to leave the country.

» What are the local laws about signing a rental agreement or owning property? Some places require a certain type of visa in order for a rental contract to be enforceable. Owning property in other countries has become more safe and reliable. However, be sure to check out the laws of your country of choice to be sure that you feel comfortable with your purchase.

Transportation

Getting around in a foreign land is always an adventure. Determining your transportation needs in advance can save you headaches and money. You will need to decide how much you can rely on public transportation or whether you will want to bring or buy a car. Here are the important factors you'll want to consider:

» How good is the public transportation in your location of choice? Some places, like most of Europe, have excellent low cost or free public transportation options. If you feel that you can reliably get to where you want to go, then it would save your budget to forego a car and just rent one when you need it. However, if you are staying in a location with few transportation options, you should look into options such as mopeds, motorcycles, and cars for reliable transportation.

» Can you bring your own car? If you plan on staying in the country for several years, it may be worth it to ship your car to your new home. However, be sure to check with their laws and regulations.

Determine if they will apply import fees, taxes, or penalties that make shipping your car impractical. Some countries will let you import a car every few years and pay minimal taxes on it. Others won't let you import any cars.

» Buy a low cost car, moped, or motorcycle. If shipping isn't an option or if you don't plan to stay in the country for more than a year, you may want to think about buying some form of transportation. Many countries have very inexpensive mopeds or motorcycles that you can purchase and then sell again when you leave. The care and maintenance of these vehicles are lower than an automobile. If there are more than two of you, a car may be the only way to go. See if you can buy a used vehicle to save on money. Choose a type of car that is common in the country, as this will mean a greater availability of both parts and mechanics if the need should arise.

If you can drive to the country where you want to live, then I would suggest you do that because it saves you a lot. However, if you are moving far, far away, the cost of shipping your car is a nightmare. It's actually cheaper for you to sell your car in your home country, move to the new country, and buy a car there. Alternatively, many expats who move to a place that has a good public transportation system don't have cars.

Most of the expats I know in Cuenca, Ecuador don't have cars, whereas those living in Playas de Rosarito or Ensenada, Baja California, Mexico do. In Cuenca, if they decide they want to drive to the coast, they rent a car. In this situation, it pays to research the road conditions because your car may not even be suitable for in-country driving. In America, we tend to have bigger cars than are allowable on the streets of other countries, especially Europe. In some Central and South American countries as well, your car won't be suitable and then you should begin to look at the cost of repairs and maintenance.

Daily Needs

The low cost of living in most second and third world countries some-times lulls expats into forgetting their budget. Even if the costs are low, little things can add up. Be sure you create an accurate list of all the things you will need on a regular basis. Here is a list of important expenses that you will need to consider for your daily needs. Other daily needs such as utilities will be addressed later:

» Groceries, cleaning supplies & sundries
» Cell phone
» Clothing
» Furnishing and home goods
» Restaurants and bars
» Entertainment, cultural events, entertaining at home
» Travel (holidays and vacations)—obviously this is not a daily expense but it's a valid need and I find it a "must have" in my budget.

Would you like a gardener or housekeeper? If your home has a pool, do you want to clean it yourself? If you want to add certain amenities to your budget, planning for them can help you get better rates and be able to afford more of them. Many of the second and third world nations offer amenities, such as spa services or housekeeping, at much lower rates than in the U.S. or Canada.

The local expat community is your best bet for learning what local delights are available at reasonable prices. They can connect you with companies and individuals who speak English. However, some services know that they can charge more for foreigners than they would the locals, especially if you require someone who speaks English. Sometimes, you can check out local prices through online websites and see if it is worth paying a little more for someone who can speak your language, or if you want to save your pennies. Once you are in the country, use the expat community to find the best and most reliable services.

We listed daily expenses including restaurants and bars. Many of you might consider that making your own meals at home will save room in your budget. That's true, but it's important to keep in mind that you are now living abroad. Certain daily comforts, such as the food you are accustomed to having in your pantry, won't always be available. Besides the problem of availability, the cost might not be what you're accustomed to, either. America has put their little fingers into every country in the world, and you know you can find McDonald's pretty much anywhere, but it is going to cost a little more, sometimes a lot more. However, not every food is as recognizable and accessible as the fast food chain heard 'round the world.

During my time in Ecuador, I went shopping with three other expat women and they had their lists of what they were trying to find. We went to several different stores—we hired a taxi for the day—and looked for specific things. These items weren't exactly the same as they were in the States and in some stores, of course, there was a language barrier to hurdle. Plus, on top of everything else, we had to look at items with a different eye, figuring out what would be closest to the product we were actually looking for. The challenges included everything from can openers to bar stools.

When it comes to food, what you'll end up doing is going through the grocery store, trying to figure out what to get because the pasta brand you usually buy isn't available. This is another time that connecting with expats is so important because they have done all the leg work—they have found that a particular pasta is as close as you are going to come to what you get in the States or they may have found a small, out of the mainstream store that caters to foreign taste buds and you can actually get A-1 Sauce. (Mercado Del Mar in Rosarito has it and it's a tiny little store—except for the back room that has over 90 kinds of Tequila!)

Another difference I've encountered has to do with what's "normal". At one point I found myself craving a candy bar. I just wanted a regular, old American candy bar and I went to the little shop on the corner and, indeed, they had Snickers candy bars. And each bar cost $2.50. This being for a standard size Snickers, not even the jumbo size! Why? Because it's imported and by the time all the tax is added to it, something that in the U.S. costs eighty-nine cents costs a couple bucks. In contrast, if I want to buy the local ice cream, rather than imported brands I'm familiar with, it's going to be a lot less than what I pay for ice cream in the States. It will always depend on what the item is and how in-demand it will be. Unless you are living close to the border of a country that has a lot of similar items to what you are used to, you have got to get creative and say, "OK, so I want pasta, this is the local pasta. I will try it. If I don't like it, I will try a different one." Psst.. If you don't like the pasta, you can always start pleading with relatives to ship you care packages of your favorites until you find something new to take its place.

What about "getting outta Dodge" for a while?

Something to keep in mind as an expat is that travel and vacations are perceived a little differently when living abroad. There is a saying about vacations that goes, "instead of planning your next vacation, why not plan a life you don't need to escape from."

This is a concept embraced by a lot of expats. While you're not on permanent vacation, you are creating a new life in a new, exotic (to you) place. Vacationing becomes more for the cultural aspects of exploring, rather than escaping. Many expats going on 'vacation' will travel to places for things that their city doesn't have an abundance of; things such as art museums or cultural events or maybe even good hiking trails for those living in more urban areas.

In Baja, for example, people will travel to take part in whale watching. There is a "path", not too far offshore, paralleling the west coast that the whales travel down, starting in late fall, early winter. You can see the spouts shoot out of the water and you'll know that the whales are migrating south, traveling towards southern Baja to give birth. Once the calves (baby whales) are ready, the migration begins that takes them back to the northern waters they call home. What that means during these migration periods for folks living in Mexico, especially Baja, is that it's time to go whale watching. There are boat tours that take visitors to areas where the mother whales like to bring their calves because the water is warmer. And this is where you can have the incredible experience of having the moms push their calves up to the surface, even close enough to the boats so that people can actually touch them.

For most of these vacations, whether it's whale watching in Baja, visiting art galleries in Cuenca, or sampling the goods at wineries in Argentina, if these are areas that are nearby to where you are living as an expat, the prices of these "vacations" are cheaper than prices in the U.S.

Another possibility for a vacation is a cruise. If embarking on a cruise from the Port of Ensenada, Mexico, for example, it is possible to find a trip for half the price of what customers leaving from, say, Los Angeles are going to pay. Keep in mind that if you board cruises in Spanish (or French, etc.) speaking countries, you may find that is the primary language of the cruise and you'll need to adjust. On many of the expat forums, there are people who post about all-inclusive vacations because cruise lines need to fill empty spaces. If you keep your eyes open, you can pick up an all-inclusive vacation to Acapulco or Cancun, at a fraction of the price and for a whole week.

I know, I know, so many choices, so little time. That's one of the very fun parts of being both retired and an expat. There are just so many fun things to do.

And now back to the more mundane and equally important pieces of the budget.

Utilities

Besides the major expense of housing, utilities such as electric, gas, and water are going to have a large impact on your budget. These expenses are also not necessarily going to be what you are familiar with in the States. For example, electricity is going to cost you more in southern locations, like Mexico, than it is in the States. Prices will vary according to country, making it important to exhaust your resources when researching and then comparing location to location.

Keep in mind that, when living in a second or third world country, the reliability of electricity isn't guaranteed.

Individually, you may have problems with your building's electricity, because of faulty wiring or older systems, but in some cases entire cities may go down. The weather in other countries plays a different part depending on the infrastructure systems these cities employ. For example, in the two and a half years I have been in Rosarito, the entire city's electricity went down once. I lost the electricity at my apartment on one occasion because of the wiring and another time my housing complex went down twice in one afternoon for two hours. That particular afternoon was very blustery and it had been storming on and off close to the coast. Surprisingly, it was the inland areas that were the real concern because that's where the city's transformers are located.

Like many coastal areas, Rosarito has a microclimate, where a mile away there could be a completely different weather situation. Although this particular storm wasn't all that bad where I was, my electricity went down because of the city's power grid. This is one of those times when I was very relieved to have a gas stove and plenty of candles, because I could still use the stove for cooking and also create a bit of light for myself with the candles.

Water is also very important to research. Can you rely on the local tap water or will you need to build buying water into your budget? The quality of the water depends on where you are; Ecuador is a classic example of these differences. You can drink the water in Cuenca right out of the tap; you do not drink the tap water in Salinas (or anywhere else along the coast or in the Amazon). There, you only drink filtered water and you only get ice cubes that are made with filtered water. It's important to know enough Spanish to ask the wait staff if filtered water is used to wash vegetables, and just don't order anything you have any hesitation over. However, in your own home and others' homes, you'll be using filtered water and, therefore, no problem.

If you intend to live in a rural area, most probably you will need to buy water. Then the question becomes whether you have it delivered to a cistern or buy 5 gallon bottles that you take into town for refilling or some other solution. This is where connecting with expats can be very helpful as water is truly the elixir of life and you need to know you have access to the good stuff.

Just remember, when it comes to water, do your research. Contact expats who are living where you are considering and get their input, figure out what you need to do (if anything), and what it will cost to put it in your budget, and go from there.

It's important to be aware and observant and to also create your own way of handling water issues so that you can lead a normal life. People all over the planet deal with these issues and we can, too.

Insurance

Many people have a handful of varying types of insurance in the States. A list might contain homeowner's insurance, flood insurance, renter's insurance, accident insurance, car insurance, to name a few.

What happens when you move abroad?

Well, that all depends. Where are you going? What are the laws there? What do you actually need versus what you're used to having? What do you need to keep active in your home country?

This subject will require you to do research because everywhere is different.

Obviously, if you are not driving a car, motorcycle, scooter, etc., you don't need insurance for your vehicle. If you are, then you'd need to make time to check out the regulations for where you intend to live. In Mexico, if you are driving and don't have car insurance, you could be arrested if the Policia pull you over. It's the law and they don't see it as a subject for negotiation. I always have my proof of insurance with me, just as I do in the States. And that needs to be factored into your budget, both the insurance in your home country (if needed) and in your new country (if needed). I pay about $275 per year for Mexican insurance. In Ecuador, it's considerably more and you have to really look for a company that will insure your vehicle. There, the only required insurance is something called SOAT that covers emergency medical expenses and, at last check, costs well under $100 per year.

As you can see, these are only two countries and they have very different laws. You can find a lot of the information you need by searching the Internet. And again, this is where connecting with expats is very helpful. They can tell you what you need and recommend companies to provide coverage.

Think about what other kinds of insurance you might need and then find out if it's available where you are considering going and how much it will cost.

Just an aside, and something to keep in mind, most countries are run by civil law as opposed to common law. As a non-lawyer, the way I explain it is that if someone buys a bowl of soup in a restaurant, spills it and burns herself, in the U.S. (common law) that restaurant could be successfully sued for amazing amounts of money. When the exact same thing happens in a civil law country, the wait staff would be very solicitous, help as quickly as possible, make any phone calls needed, and then ask if she would like a fresh bowl of soup, end of story. Obviously, this is very simplistic and any lawyer reading this will probably have seventeen fits. However, I think it gets the point across. Common law means one can use discretionary powers to decide (among other things) and civil law means decisions are based on what the law is as it is written. To break it down even more: in common law, you can be sued without legal document previously allowing the lawsuit. In civil law, you cannot sue without a contract.

DON'T LET ME BE MISUNDERSTOOD

CHAPTER FOUR: LANGUAGE

For some people the idea of living in a country that uses a different language can bring up fear and anxiety. For others, they may think it isn't that big a deal and are fully prepared to either learn it or bluff their way along with some basic vocabulary. As mentioned earlier, communication can become a challenge when you have little or no skills in the language of your new country. The simplest things become huge obstacles because you aren't able to clearly express yourself and what it is you need help with. I remember when I was trying to ask a non-English speaking man if he was the person who refilled my large water bottle, because I needed to pay for it. I finally just gave him the money and hoped for the best. Fortunately, he was the right person and I knew how to handle it in the future. I was lucky this was a small incident that would have cost me only a few pesos if I had made a mistake. What it brought home to me is that I needed to improve my language skills so that I can manage, at least, a basic level of conversation in a variety of situations.

If you are lucky enough to have an intermediate level of your new language, then you are a step ahead. Be sure to keep learning and practicing every chance you get. It will make a huge difference in how quickly you can acclimate to your new environment and will come in very handy when you are faced with any type of emergency or frustrating situation.

Learning the Language

What I want to provide to you in this chapter is an overview of learning another language. There are a variety of ways to approach it and you should definitely consider how you learn best.

To begin with, there are several very important language issues you want to consider. First, you need to know local idioms, phrases, and pronunciation to avoid cultural faux pas and to get along with your neighbors. An example in Spanish is the word using the letters "a n o". When there is a ˜ over the "n" (año), it means year and is pronounced as if it were spelled "annyo". When there is no ˜ (ano), it is pronounced just the way it's spelled, ano, and means anus. As you can imagine, that's quite a difference and can cause some embarrassment if pronounced incorrectly.

Before we go any further, I want to make sure you understand that even if you are moving to a place that uses your own language, there can be some really big differences in how words are used. I shall now relate a most embarrassing moment that occurred for me in Australia. I was at a party and we were talking about sports and the subject of golf came up. I said that, although I don't actually play the game, I was raised in a family where both my parents played. As a matter of fact, sometimes my dad would want to practice at the field across the street and I'd go out and shag his balls. To say this brought down the house is putting it mildly. I grew up with a Midwestern U.S. vocabulary and what I said meant I'd go pick up all the golf balls after my dad had hit them. In Australia, it meant something entirely different and I turned beet red when I learned what it was. So it's also important to learn how vocabulary is used in your new location, even when it's the same language.

Another aspect to consider is making sure your vocabulary can handle basic information on plumbing, basic repairs, or public utility issues. Most importantly you will want to gain a fluency that will allow you to communicate with a doctor or police officer in case of an emergency. Relying on dictionaries and a smattering of high school language classes might work when you are trying to find a restroom or haggle over a souvenir, but in a critical moment, knowing the language can make the difference between getting what you need and huge frustration.

Styles of Learning

So, what's a person to do? Is there one quick and easy way to becoming fluent? Don't we wish! Fortunately, there are many approaches to learning a language. The method you choose depends on you, your learning style, how much time you have, and your sense of adventure.

Let me break down your options from easy and quick to thorough and intensive. Each method has benefits and drawbacks that will be listed at the end of each section. It's up to you to determine which method is best for your situation.

#1 Living By the Seat of Your Pocket Guides

The simplest and most iffy way to start is to buy a traveler's dictionary, head to your country of choice and spend your time self-teaching, wandering the country with smiles and gestures. This method is for people who may not have time to take a class or whose learning style functions best under pressure. Another type of person who would use this language style is one who never intends to learn the language. I met a guy who lives in Mexico and had never learned the language. He specifically chose a location where he could get along using English exclusively. He lives in a gated community that is pretty much all American and Canadian expats. Even with this type of lifestyle, it would be good to have something to fall back on when you need help from a local. A pocket dictionary can help.

Whether you don't want to learn the language or you are an adventurous self-starter, here are a few options for pocket guides that go beyond the average language dictionary:

Internet Options

If you have Internet access, on your phone or computer, there are free language translation websites offered by Yahoo!, Google and other sites. Do a search for your language and include the word "translation". Here are two sites to get you started: http://babelfish.yahoo.com or http://translate.google.com.

Of course, accessing the Internet isn't always practical when you are out and about, so try...

There's an App for That!

Most smart phones or PDA's, such as Android, iPad and iPhone, have translation applications that you can download. Simply type in the word, phrase or short sentence and it will translate it into the language of your choice. These applications even offer audio so that you can hear how the words are pronounced. Even better, most of the apps are free! Check out the following free apps available for most smart phones: BabelFish Voice, Google Translate, Flashcards and more (in a variety of languages). *Hint - Make sure that you have signed your phone up for local phone service so that it is working when you need it.*

Language Translators

You can buy pocket language translators—hand-held mini-computers that act much as the free phone apps do. Simply type in a word or phrase and it will speak the translation to you. I' found them ranging in price from $19.95 to over $400. Some are just text and others have audio/video capabilities. One of the benefits of using the language translator is that it doesn't need Internet or local phone service. It's both portable and easy to use.

If you plan to live by the seat of your pocket guide, these devices can be much more helpful and quick to use than trying to page back and forth through a dictionary.

Pocket Guide Summary:

Benefits of the Pocket Guides:

» Quick and Easy.

» No courses or long-term training commitments.

» If your phone application or translator offers an audio component, it will actually help you learn the language as you use it.

» This is a great option if your style is to learn as you go.

» These applications and translators, with their audio pronunciation of the words, will offer better command of the language than thumbing through a dictionary.

Drawbacks of the Pocket Guides:

» In emergencies, when you may need to be quick and also convey information that is not commonplace, e.g., about stroke, heart attack, broken bones, etc., a guide will be slow, cumbersome and, possibly, inaccurate.

» Slow for daily use.

» Typing in phrases each day will get old very quickly.

» Plus you run the risk of bad translations or incorrect usage, which can be embarrassing.

#2 Going It Alone - Audio & Video Self-Study

If you want something more formal than just learning as you go, but less time intensive than formal classes, then try self-study programs. There are several varieties, ranging in price and intensity. The easiest are the audio programs that you can put in your CD or MP3 player. The next level of training are the many audio/video programs available on computer. Finally, Internet based training also offers a variety of programs from simple audio to online tutoring programs.

Audio Programs

You can learn a lot through audio language programs, if you have the discipline. Audio Language programs are great for quick, low cost learning. It is especially a good idea if you drive or travel a lot, or have time to listen frequently. Simply pop the CD or audio file into your player then listen and practice imitating the words. Some people even use head phones while they sleep—listening to the audio in this relaxed state will allow the brain to absorb the accents and inflections of the language.

Audio/Visual Programs

There are many audio/visual-learning programs available for computer use. These programs offer a deeper learning process because they allow you to see and hear the word, usually associating it with a video or images. Because this method uses more of your senses, you learn more quickly. The drawback to these programs is that you must be on your computer to use them. That means you must set aside consistent training times in order to see the benefits.

Online Training Programs

Many of the online training programs are set up like the audio/visual programs and let you go at your own pace. Others offer live training and private tutoring through an online environment. Having training with a live person gives you a more accurate understanding of the speed you will hear the language spoken in daily life. Many of the audio and visual programs slow the speech down considerably to help you learn. With a live, online instructor, you will hear the words spoken more realistically.

Self-study programs can be much less expensive and quicker to use. I suggest you check your local library. They may have some of the courses available to try before buying it for yourself.

Self-Study Summary:

Benefits of Self-study:

» Low cost and time-flexible.

» You get to plug in your training time around your schedule.

» Most of these courses are reasonably priced, ranging from $19.95 to $500.

» You can choose the level at which you need to learn and learn what you want to learn, ignoring the phrases or topics which are less important to you.

» Online classes can give you the flexibility of self-study, combined with the more natural approach of a live instructor.

Drawbacks of Self-study:

» It requires you to be completely self-motivated and consistent.

» If you tend to get distracted when you're in front of a computer, you know, checking email, reading the latest blogs or playing games, then you might find you've wasted your money.

» Another consideration is that audio files, though less expensive and easier, are less effective than the audio/video.

Both types of self-study have varying levels of quality. Stiff forms of speaking and less than practical examples are the most common complaints of self-study classes. Be sure to read independent reviews before shelling out any money for a program. The same goes for online learning, which can be far more expensive and glitchy. Make sure they are known for having a clear Internet connection and fast download speeds or dealing with software issues will eat up most of your class time.

#3 Getting Face-to-Face

It might be that you need a more personal or structured experience to learn a language. Whether you join classes that require you to show up and do homework, or language groups that provide a more natural learning environment, there are a number of options for face-to-face learning.

Classes

One obvious approach to learning another language is through a local school. You can take courses at a community college, adult learning annex, or private language school. It is easy to find these classes in the phone book under Language Schools or by searching terms such as "learn Spanish Denver Colorado" (using the language and location you want) to find programs in your area. The options can range from a simple language class to advanced offerings. With most classes, you will need to be able to dedicate time for the regularly scheduled classes.

Tutors

If you need a more flexible schedule for your training program, a tutor is the way to go. You can hire a language tutor through most language schools. Your tutor can work with your schedule to find times that are right for you. This method of training also has the benefit of one-on-one training. So if you are shy or have trouble learning languages, a tutor is a more private format and can help you gradually overcome fears and stumbling blocks.

Language Groups

Language groups are less structured than classes or tutoring because they are usually just a group of language users who come together to practice. This is not a good option for those who have no background in the subject, but is great for those who have taken some classes and need to refresh their skills. You can find these groups online through sites like meetup.com, Yahoo groups, or just do a search for "Spanish language practice groups Denver Colorado", again using the language of interest and your location. Most of them are free or offered by an instructor for a small fee.

Face-to-Face Summary:

Benefits of Face-to-Face:

» This type of training offers you a more natural way of conversing in the language.

» You'll also get a more regular, consistent, and correct education.

» Having an instructor or language speaker available to answer your questions will help you gain a deeper understanding of the language.

Drawbacks of Face-to-Face:

» The price can be high and there will be constraints on your time.

» Classes can be dogmatic and inflexible if you want to focus your learning on a specific area of the language.

» Tutoring can be even more costly and some tutors can be flaky. Be sure to check references.

» Language groups are hit and miss. Some are highly active and educational and others are sporadic, cliquish, or unprofessional.

#4 Swimming the Deep Waters - Full Immersion

One fun, though sometimes daunting, option is called immersion training. Immersion is done in a variety of ways; from classes taught solely in the language you are learning, to full cultural immersion that places you with a school, family or group within a country that uses that language.

Class Immersion

These classes can be taken before you head off to your country of choice. Taught locally, they do all of their instruction while speaking the language you are learning. This can be difficult if you have a question, because the instructor will want you to ask the question in that language and will provide the answer in that language. It can feel a bit overwhelming at first, but it is a very quick and efficient way to learn. Many schools that offer immersion classes also offer them in one or two week blocks of time, or at an off-site location. So instead of a weekly training class, you would go to a camp or school where everyone, the staff and students alike, will be speaking the language. In an off-site program, you stay in the training facility overnight and for a specific length of time, usually a weekend or one to two weeks. This complete immersion trains your brain to speak, think and live that language.

In-country, Class Immersion

Though similar to the off-site programs mentioned above, these in-country programs offer the added benefit of being located in the country where the language is spoken. The school can then take their students out into the "real world" environment where they can experience speaking the language and learning local customs, idioms, and accents.

Cultural Exchange & Immersion

These programs are in just about every country. You live with a family for a specified period of time and the only language that is spoken is that of the country where you're now living. The advantage here is that you will be in a safe environment to learn and your host family understands that you are a beginner and will spend time helping you with your vocabulary and grammar. I have a friend who, as a retiree, went to Mexico for six weeks on an immersion program and loved it. Another friend went to Japan for a year abroad while in college. She lived with a family and became fluent in Japanese and got around quite well. The challenge for her was that she learned her language mostly from the two sons. In the Japanese language there is a difference in the vocabulary and grammar for males and females and she learned the male version. During the summer she worked for me, she also worked at a Japanese restaurant. At one point, while she was serving a group of Japanese businessmen and she spoke with them in their language, they were quite put out with her because she was not speaking as a woman should. One can get into the whole conversation about the "why". The purpose for relating this story is to point out that one can innocently misspeak and experience quite unintended consequences.

If you search the term 'language immersion programs', you'll find a variety of options. One that offers a wide range of countries is:

LanguagesAbroad.com - http://www.languagesabroad.com/

Even if this isn't the right program for you, the information on their site will be useful as you consider any program. Remember that all immersion programs will charge a fee so be sure to look around and find what works for you. It's also important that you ask for references. If the organization will not let you contact anyone who has been through their program, I'd be highly suspicious and tell them so. And keep looking for a program that is open and welcoming to you.

Another website that is very useful in helping pick an immersion program is AmeriSpan. Here's a link to their page that provides some very good points to consider when choosing where you want to go.

AmeriSpan - http://www.amerispan.com/language_schools/choosing. asp

Deep Waters Summary

Benefits of Full Immersion:

» The fastest way for your mind to grasp the language is through immersion.

» Combining travel to your country of choice with an in-country immersion program can be both fun, educational, and an excellent way to "try on" a location before committing to moving there.

» You'll learn more about the country and customs because these programs often teach the country's culture and history, as well as their local business and government information.

» Cultural exchange immersion programs provide you with immediate friends and helpers, a family or group that lives in the country and can help you acclimate to its culture and daily activities.

Drawbacks of Full Immersion:

» It can be overwhelming for someone who has not had any prior language experience.

» Immersion programs can be costly, so make sure to check them out thoroughly and check referrals.

» A much greater time commitment, as you will need to have time for classes and travel.

Regardless of how you go about learning your new language, it's critical to become basically competent. You'll be able to have conversations with interesting people and feel part of the community. Proper training in your new country's language can help you avoid stepping on toes, giving you a proper understanding of conduct and customs. Most important of all, becoming fluent helps keep you safe and able to handle unexpected emergencies.

CHANGES IN LATITUDES, CHANGES IN ATTITUDES

CHAPTER FIVE: CULTURAL ADAPTATION

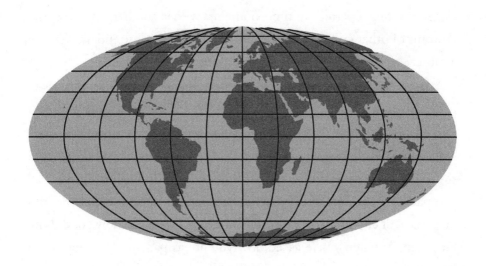

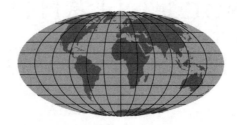

DO YOU ENJOY THE UNEXPECTED? DO YOU HANDLE LONG LINES, SLOW workers, and miscommunications with aplomb or at least a good sense of humor? No? Then you are like a lot of other people. One of the big challenges to moving abroad is dealing with the changes, cultural differences, and bureaucracies of your new country. This chapter will help you prepare for the changes and lower your stress level.

Am I Cut Out for This?

Relocating one's life isn't for everyone. Who are the best candidates for a successful transition? Someone who has done a lot of traveling, not just tours, but longer periods of time. Someone who is familiar with accepting customs of other cultures. Someone who is not quick to judgment when another's actions don't fit with expectations.

Americans moving abroad tend to congregate in relatively close proximity, often creating little pockets that are somewhat similar to what they had back home. When that happens, the need to embrace change is a bit tempered. However, those who keep to themselves and don't spend time with their new community tend to become disillusioned. After all, isn't part of living abroad about the new experiences that it offers? Besides, no place will end up being "just like home" and that's a really good thing. Surprisingly, when you're asked how you are as part of a greeting, you'll find that people will genuinely care and listen to your answer.

What a breath of fresh air!

Social Interaction

Whether you are going to an American movie with German voice-overs, conversing with friends on the piazza, or dancing the samba in a local club—one of the most fun parts about visiting overseas is learning about new cultures.

Unfortunately, what is fun when you are visiting for a few weeks can be quite a culture shock when you live there day in and day out. While you may find yourself overwhelmed with all the changes in your new land, there are a few areas that might need some major adjustment:

» Food

» Politics

» Religion

» Sports

» Behavior/body language

» Medicine

Food

Mmm... The baklava, the fried plantain, the braised lamb's tongue, and lung stew – wait, what? One of the cultural differences that you will experience daily is the food. If you are adventurous, this could be an exciting time with all the new tastes and textures. However, three to six months down the road you may be surprised at what foods from home you are craving. After three months in Greece, a friend of mine had had enough of lamb to last a lifetime. What she wouldn't have given for a cheeseburger, fries, and a Coke... and she didn't even eat those very often back home.

Here are some ways to prevent food burnout or food faux pas and stay interested in the food of your new country:

Just-Like-Home Night

Have at least one night a week where you make a traditional dinner from your home or childhood. Sometimes finding the ingredients can be a hassle, so you might want to bring enough dry ingredients for your favorite dish for the first few weeks. After that, maybe you can get friends to ship care packages to you.

Local Hangouts

Find the local hangouts that serve food from your country. Contact local expats for recommendations. Many have websites, Facebook groups, or Yahoo! Groups to keep connected.

New Favorites

Create a list of your favorite foods of your new country and have them at hand for snacking.

Ask Questions

Make sure you know what you are asking for when ordering off a menu. Try to find menus with pictures. Be sure to ask what is included in the meal or you may get something you do not recognize. While in Australia, I had an interesting hamburger experience. My friend and I were sitting in a small café, with no other customers there. In walks an American couple and the woman orders a cheeseburger. She complains so the waiter asks her what she ordered and when she tells him, he says to her, "That's what you have, a cheeseburger." In Australia the typical cheeseburger has the following: burger patty, cheese, shredded beets, shredded carrots, sometimes cucumber, sometimes bacon, sometimes a fried egg, no condiments such as mustard, catsup, lettuce, tomato or pickle. If you absolutely have to have a burger like what you'd find in the States, go to the local McDonald's – they're everywhere. I've also heard of people in Italy ordering a pizza, who were then served a piece of toast with a slice of mozzarella and a tomato on top.

Local Customs

Find out what the local customs are when eating in social situations. In some countries it is offensive to leave food on your plate, while in others, a clean plate means you want more. Others require that you belch after a meal as a compliment to the cook.

Support

There is a support structure built in as you become an expat. Yes, you have your family rooting for you and sitting by their email, eagerly awaiting an update from you. But what is important to keep in mind is that the people already living in your new location are excellent sources of support. There are a variety of folks you can tap into:

- » Family – maybe you have relatives who are living in your new location
- » Expat community
- » Landlord/other homeowners
- » English speakers, even if you don't know them and have only heard them speak to others
- » Restaurants where local expats hang out
- » School/classes
- » Local language tutors

For this to be effective, one must be willing to venture from your new home and make the effort to go searching in the community. As easy as it is to be negative, fight it. Of course this is a struggle, but embrace it and watch how you adapt. Try your hardest not to be whiney to your support groups. It's so easy to nitpick, when in reality we can appreciate all these obstacles as hurdles we will overcome to create a new, beautiful life. If your family is only hearing you talk about the negative aspects, they will reflect negativity back to you and, in turn, you will only carry that negativity into your new relationships.

When Don and I lived in Paris, it was the first time for both of us. We were excited to explore and collect experiences. Our landlord, Dawn, called us the first week we were there to make sure everything was working out with our apartment. The conversation was fairly short but still created a tentative connection. She called again the second week and we had a marvelous conversation, getting all kinds of suggestions for grocery shopping, laundry, cafes, and other tidbits, along with much sharing of personal stories. As a result, Dawn invited Don and me to visit with her and her husband, Dominique who went by Dom, for a long weekend in Roubaix. We had a marvelous time with them and I was just glad my name is Ann.

Bottom line…Exhaust your resources.

Talk to everyone who seems like they're familiar with the area and willing to teach you a thing or two. Meet your neighbors, frequent the local restaurants, and make yourself familiar with the stores in your vicinity. Most people are friendly and want to help, especially when you make the effort to speak in their language. You'll be surprised how far people will go to help when you show them your interest in learning their language.

Talking with an expat in Medellin, Colombia, she told me about an amazing experience she had. Apparently, she was new to Medellin and had just walked out to the corner and was looking around, trying to figure out which way to go to get to a particular place. A local woman came up to her and asked if she could help. The expat told her what she was looking for and the local couldn't help her. However, she had a friend who could, so she got her to come over and join the conversation. The second local knew where the place was and asked the expat if it would be okay if she walked her over to the store, which they proceeded to do. All this happened because the brand new expat was willing to accept help when it was offered.

There is a word of caution here: you still need to pay close attention to your gut when meeting and talking with people. We tend to trust others who are from the same country as ourselves. And just like at home, there are those who are out to take us for a ride. They speak English, they have the same citizenship, and they know the expat community will trust them. In this situation, apply the same protections you use back home and be sure to trust your gut. Although most of us have honed our survival skills over the years, we seem to leave some of them at the border. So be aware and use the same intelligence and caution that you used back home when deciding whom to trust and bring into your new "family".

Of course, I have to share one story about an expat who wasn't what she presented. I'll call her Vanessa. She had a lovely dog named Charlie and since I also had a couple of dogs, we tended to run into each other when out walking them. We chatted frequently, and then began having lunch together. At one point she talked about a business she wanted to start, and since I love big picture thinking, we knocked around some ideas. At one point she asked me if I'd like to work with her in putting this idea into practice. I told her that I was headed in another direction so I wasn't interested. Not too long after that conversation, Vanessa was arrested and extradited to the U.S. as a fugitive from San Diego. She had fled the country when she was out on bail, awaiting trial for insurance fraud and then Tweeted "catch me if you can" using her real name. Talk about dodging the bullet! She had been tried in absentia, found guilty, and sentenced to 20 years in prison. Alas, I was unable to learn what happened to her lovely dog. At any rate, it is important to pay attention and trust yourself.

All that being said, do remember that for the most part, other expats are where they are because it suits them and they've chosen their new home. They have much to share and can make your transition so, so much easier. The same can be said of most of the people you will meet in your new locale. If you reach out to them in an open and friendly way, they usually reciprocate.

Expat Community

We've just been over the importance of a support system for adapting to a new culture, and you may be wondering if it's entirely necessary to familiarize yourself with the expat community. Wouldn't the real adventure just be to dive into the local mixture and really get a sense of the place? An expat community is so valuable; there is almost no price to put on it. There are so many things we don't know that we *don't know* about a new location. People who are already living there can help with those things. More than just living there, these are people who have gone through the same struggle you are just beginning.

When I first moved to Rosarito, Baja California, Mexico, I often traveled back north across the border to the San Diego area. This also raised the question for me of where I would want to be treated in case of a medical emergency, or even for routine medical appointments. What I learned from talking to expats was that if I had a medical directive (not a legal document) from a Mexican doctor that stated that I needed to go to San Diego for treatment, I could then have access to what is called the Fast Lane to cross back into the US. This can make a huge difference in how long it takes to pass through Immigration.

What it boils down to is that by tapping into the expat community, there is much that can be alleviated as you get used to your new environment. And without that community, certain things will be so much more challenging. Even if you already speak the native language well enough to ask questions of the locals, there are still things they won't know about, because they have not had to deal with them – such as medical treatment documents for crossing the border.

Resources for how to find an expat community are included in Appendix I.

Politics

What is that saying... don't speak of religion, income, or politics in polite company? Be prepared! The rules of politics and speaking about politics can be positively haywire (from your perspective) in other countries.

While the U.S. and Canada are political nations, other countries can seem almost obsessive about politics and yet others never speak about it. Plus, their politics might include bashing the politics of your home country. What can you do about it?

First, stay calm. It will not help matters if you get angry. Depending on who you are listening to, you may choose to just ignore it. Taxi drivers, or people on the street, can be ignored. Better yet, tell them how wise they are and you will win a friend who may later listen to your side of things. Sometimes the political comments will come from work associates or friends. Listen conscientiously. Just because you love your country doesn't mean it hasn't made a mistake or two. Point out that you understand their point of view. Once the other person is satisfied they have been heard, they will probably back off of the conversation.

The most important thing to remember is that you are in their country. Be respectful of the fact that they see things from a different perspective. If you try to convince them that they are wrong or that your country did the right thing, without fully listening to their argument, you will lose the battle, and a possible friend. *Or maybe not.* In some countries, heated political battles are common dinner conversation. It is considered good form to battle it out. You need to understand the culture you are living in and make adjustments accordingly.

A word of caution to U.S. citizens – you will learn that, generally speaking, citizens of other countries know considerably more about the U.S. than people in the U.S. know about other countries. Why? Because the U.S. has been the world leader in so many ways (good and bad) for so long that it is in the best interests of other countries to be well educated about the U.S. When I spent time in Australia, I learned that it took about twenty minutes for people to ask me a question about why some political action or some particular crime occurred in the U.S. And, sometimes, they knew more about it than I did.

Religion

This is a very important and very tricky subject in any country. It behooves you as an expat to understand how religion is viewed in whatever country you intend to live for any period of time. It is not uncommon for a country to have one dominant religion. What that means for you, as an expat, is to understand yourself in regards to religion. If you have strong viewpoints on your own religion and it is different than the dominant religion of your chosen location, will that be a problem? If you think it might, perhaps it would be better to find a location where the people have beliefs similar to yours or are open to many religious beliefs.

If you would like to know if your specific religion has a presence in a location you're considering, there are a couple ways you can research that. Certainly one way is talk to your minister/rabbi/priest/mullah/etc. and ask if they know or, if they don't, who you might contact to find out. Another way is to do an online search using the name of your religion and the name of the city or country that is your destination of interest. Then contact anyone who you identify living in that location and practicing your religion. Ask them what it's like to be living there and any other questions you may have.

What's very important, and I've no doubt you already know this, is that we are always respectful of the local beliefs, even if they are not our own. We are guests in any country we move to and, as such, we need to not be on a mission to make it "just like home". We certainly don't have to switch our beliefs to theirs, just as they don't need to change theirs to ours.

Sports

I would not have thought about sports as any big deal... until I started spending time in other countries. What I found was that, depending on the country, they can be ardent fans of a sport I have no interest in, or worse, a sport that I am totally opposed to.

What I learned is that it's important to be aware of how a culture thinks about their sports. Other countries may have different ideas about what is right or moral. There are some sports, such as dog, cock, or bull fighting or perhaps, fox hunting, which are illegal where you come from and are legal and well attended in your new locale. You do not have to participate or attend these functions unless you want to. If anyone asks you why you don't go, answer calmly that it isn't your thing. However, getting upset and condemning a sport that is important to the people of that culture will not win you any friends.

Also, keep in mind that some countries are truly fanatical about a particular sport, such as soccer or cricket. It would endear you to your neighbors if you try to learn a little bit about the sport and occasionally participate with them in the excitement of game day.

Behavior and Body Language

Using the wrong gesture or word is often the biggest source of misunderstanding and laughter when you are in another country. Even English speaking countries have differences of language and behavior that can cause amusing situations. For example, asking someone to pass a napkin at a restaurant in Australia will get you some mighty strange looks. The first floor in England is not the same floor in America.

So imagine how confusing things get when you add in another language, plus body language. In parts of South America it is proper to point at people with your middle finger. In Greece, a nod up means no. In some Middle Eastern countries, passing something with your left hand is considered an insult. So do your research. Find out what strange quirks of speech and body language are important in your new home.

This is especially true if you plan to do business. It is critical that you understand the social mores, idioms, issues of time and protocol, and much more. Misunderstandings in this area could be as serious as a loss of respect and customers, or as amusing as expecting a shipment of leather and getting a wild pig instead.

One of the great ways to learn about these things quickly is to meet up with the local expats in the area. Most cities have small clusters of people who have moved there from other countries. They can tell you all the horror stories and stop you from making the same mistakes. There are many books and online resources that can provide you with a clearer picture of social mores, body language and cultural idiosyncrasies. Appendix 1 provides links to a variety of useful resources.

"I Need Home" Moments

We'll go over keeping connected with your family and friends later in the guide, but what happens when a dose of your family and friends just isn't enough? What if you find yourself needing a bit of the "old homeland"? You miss the lack of language barrier, the speedy work ethic, the ease of going to the grocery story and locating your favorite food, the reliable utilities, and the comforts of the familiar. In many cases, most people won't be in immediate reach of crossing the border back into their home country. When this happens, make the effort to turn to your new home for support. Turn to the expat community for support; they've been in your shoes! Locate chain restaurants where you can order off of a familiar menu (you'll be surprised by how many there are…and they aren't all McDonald's); check out local movie theaters that are showing movies being advertised at home (and find out when/if there are certain showings that will be in English); find a club or bar that carries on the familiar traditions, like Monday night football or World Soccer Cup finals.

A Change of Heart

Before we leave this chapter, it's important to address a very important concern of many who are considering this exciting adventure of living abroad.

What happens when you move to your new country and it's not everything you dreamed it would be? We've been talking about the cultural differences and challenges and maybe they are just too much for you. Or maybe you miss your friends and family too much or the lifestyle isn't what you expected. Here are a few tips that can help:

Create a Strong Social Circle

It's hard to miss home when you are busy having a good time. Usually, homesickness happens because you haven't made friends and found interesting things to do. So get out there! Join groups or organizations that have fun events you like. Find the local expat hangout and talk with other people who have gone through the same experiences and come out the other side. Choose happy people because unhappy ones will just reinforce your negative feelings. Once you have met some people you like, make an effort to see them regularly. Start a game night or movie day. Create a standing lunch date. If you are single, check out the online international and expat dating websites to find singles in your area. It will take some effort to get you out of your doldrums but you came here for the adventure -- so go out and find it.

Remember Why You Wanted to Move

When you were thinking about moving abroad, did you have dreams of all the things you would do in your new home? Well... are you doing them? It's amazing how we sometimes get bogged down by the day-to-day living and forget to go out and enjoy ourselves. Grab your tour book and make a point to visit all those places you wanted to visit. If you have visited them all, then find the hidden gems. Ask the locals about interesting locations that may not be in the guidebooks. They can tell you about restaurants, open markets, historical monuments, crumbling ruins, fantastic salsa clubs, and much more.

Make it Your Home

Sometimes we are so excited when we first arrive that we don't take care of the details of our life. If the changes have been coming at you too fast, then take a break to integrate your experiences. Take a weekend and do nothing but decorate your home, apartment or room. Combine the pieces of your old life with objects from your new life. Clear out the clutter and unpack those boxes. Do the mundane housework that you've been putting off. Taking time to go within and take care of the details of your life can help your mind adjust to the idea that you are not just on a long vacation -- you are home.

Connecting or Disconnecting

Balance your new life with your old. Are you taking time to connect with your friends and family back home or are you connecting too much with people back home and not with anyone local? Evaluate where you are on the spectrum. Homesickness can sometimes be assuaged by re-connecting with family, care-packages from home, and brief visits to or from friends. However, if you have more interaction with the people back home than with your new life, then you may need to disconnect for a time. Tell your friends and family that you are going to take a break or cut down on interaction so that you can more fully integrate yourself with your new life. Then find clubs and groups to join. Give it time. Starting new friendships can take awhile. The reward is that, when you make the effort and begin connecting with people, you will feel happier in your new home.

If you try these ideas and you are still unhappy in your new home, ask yourself a simple question – why am I unhappy? Be honest with yourself.

What isn't happening that you want or thought would happen for you when you moved? The next question is – how can it be fixed? Sometimes you are happy with life, but unhappy with your living situation. Can you move to a better location? If you love the country but the culture is causing you trouble, can you find an expat group or a community that is primarily made up of your culture?

I remember talking with a gentleman who intentionally doesn't speak the language of his new country. He never plans to assimilate into the culture. Instead, he chose a gated community that caters to expats. He loves it. He has plenty of friends, and is surrounded by expats from the U.S. and Canada. He has not had to adjust much to the new culture because he hasn't really left the old one. So if that's what you are looking for, those places do exist. It's up to you to determine how much you want to interact with your new home's culture and how much you want to stay removed from it.

Here is an evaluation chart that may help you find solutions to create a happier life:

Reasons You Are Unhappy	Ideas for Change in Location, People, or Activities	What Helps and What Doesn't

Hopefully, that helped. However, if you've tried everything and are still unhappy, it's time to make some decisions.

Do you want to move back home? Maybe live in a different culture or country? Go back to the work you did in Chapter 1 to help you evaluate a better place for you to live.

As you can see, there is a diverse range of issues that can make quite a difference in how you integrate into your new environment. From legal issues to politics and medical care, you will find that research is the key to not only identifying a possible location for your expat move, it's also the key to understanding more about the culture and how you will build your community and any adaptations you may have to make. Whether you research the culture online, meet with expats who live in the area, or read guide books (hopefully, all of the above), you will be able to stop problems before they start and keep your situations positive.

Remember, it's not only about the fun parts in this new adventure; it's about the experience.

DON'T STOP ME NOW

CHAPTER SIX: GET OUT OF YOUR OWN WAY

Now that I've told you about the experience of living abroad, you are totally ready to go. You can pack up all your things and take that leap!

No?

Okay, maybe it's not that fast or easy to make that move. There are a lot of pieces to consider. Roadblocks may arise no matter the situation and no matter how much you prepare. In this chapter, we're going to give you some tips to resolve them quickly and how to navigate your way through your decisions.

So let's dig right in and find out what's holding you back from retiring abroad.

First off, what do I mean by roadblocks?

Have you ever wanted to do something and not been able to because you didn't have the time, the money, or maybe someone you love needed you to do something for them at the same time? The time, the money, or the person became the roadblock.

And did you figure out a way to still be able to do what it was you wanted so badly to do? Maybe take on a part-time job until you could save the money you needed. Or perhaps you looked at doing it another time or in a different way. Or maybe you sat down with the person who needed your help and asked if there was a way to provide what was needed in smaller chunks, a different time, or even in a completely different way.

We've all overcome roadblocks in our lives. Sometimes it's been simple – just shifting the time or place. Sometimes we've looked to others to help us overcome them.

Now it's time to do the same thing here.

Take a moment and think about it. Why haven't you made the move to retire abroad? Are there things that hold you back? Do you have worries, concerns, or frustrations?

These roadblocks may be complicated, such as commitments or responsibilities. They may be emotional as you think about digging up your roots in your community. Most often, it's about the people in our lives and the emotional nature of moving far from friends and family.

I know. I had more than a few of these on my roadblock list. When I wanted to move to Cuenca, Ecuador I had three huge roadblocks that were preventing me from pulling the trigger. See if you can relate to any of these:

The first, and most important, was my mother. She's in her nineties and has had, as you might imagine, a series of health concerns. I had to ask myself a lot of tough questions. Did I really want to be so far away from her? Could I get back to her in time, should some emergency happen? And most of all, did I want to spend these important years so far from her? It really made me hit the pause button on my moving plans. Sorting out how I could stay relatively close to her and still have the retirement of my dreams allowed me to hit the play button again. And, by the way, an emergency actually happened after I moved out of the U.S., and, because I changed where I would go (more on that later), I was able to get to her quickly.

I was in a similar situation with my dog, Tully. She was a beautiful Border Collie mix. She was also fifteen years old. There was no way I could put her in a crate and ship her to Ecuador. But she was family. I was never going to leave her behind. Tully is no longer with me as she died when she was sixteen. I never once regretted that I had changed my location so she could live out her days with me.

Finally, there was the issue of my partner's work situation. He has his own business and was not quite ready to retire from it. If I were to move to Ecuador, it would mean only seeing him a couple of times a year, until he was ready to retire. Could we live that way? Would our relationship survive the strain?

As you can see, I had some biggies!

What I discovered was that this process of identifying my roadblocks was the key to moving past them. Most of us don't sit down and identify what's holding us back. We don't want to look at them too closely because it forces us to look at the things that most of us don't want to see. We may have a vague sense of family or work obligations. We look tentatively at our budget, our house, our friendships, and wonder if it would be worth it or if we'd be making a mistake. But we don't want to put our reasons or excuses front and center. To write them down is to make them real.

Why? Because it's scary!

If you have the roadblocks in black and white, you can clearly see that a move abroad might not be in your future. At least, that's what I thought when I looked at the roadblocks that I just mentioned. I thought that there was no way I'd be leaving the country for at least another few years.

Boy, was I wrong!

In fact, it was the act of writing them down that started me thinking about solutions. So be courageous! Ask yourself the hard questions about why you are hesitating to move. There may be some important information waiting for you to uncover.

In a moment, I'm going to ask you to make a list of all those roadblocks that are holding you back. But before you do, let's consider all the different areas that may hold potential roadblocks. Some of these may be big and obvious, like mine were. Others may be smaller, but are still dragging on you. You may find that you don't have any really big roadblocks, but you have ten or more small ones that are all influencing you.

Here are some areas you will want to consider:

1. Family - Do you have a family member who needs special care? Or maybe you fear missing out on those special times with grandchildren?

2. Work - Do you still have full or part-time work? Does your spouse or partner? If you have a business, what will you do with it?

3. Finances - Can you afford to move? Would it be cost effective?

4. Health - Will the healthcare really be comparable to what you are receiving now? How about prescriptions? Will you be able to afford it?

5. Language - Do you have any foreign language skills? Are you nervous about the language issues?

6. Political Issues - Can you live in a place that may have different political views? For example: Would you be comfortable living in a socialist system of government?

7. Cultural Issues - Do you have any needs that might not be provided for in a specific culture (such as a church in your religion)? Are you comfortable in cultures that are different from your own?

8. Fears – Do you have general fears about leaving behind your old life, the safety of living abroad, or how you are going to fit in and find friends?

9. Relationships - Do you have concerns about how this will affect your friendships? Are you worried about dating? What about your pets? Will you be able to bring them and find the products and services you need to keep them healthy?

10. Commitments/Responsibilities - Are there any responsibilities that you have, such as caring for members of your family? Maybe you have been the person who traditionally hosts the holiday parties? Are you involved in a volunteer position?

I know that may seem like a lot of things to think about. But don't worry – you'll be looking at how to overcome the roadblocks later. For right now, take a deep breath and dig into those potential roadblocks that are holding you back. Make a list of them here:

Some roadblocks that are holding me back are...

1. _____

2. _____

3. _____

4. _____

5. _____

6. _____

7. _____

Bringing those feelings, issues, and problems into the daylight may not be easy, but it will allow you to start searching for solutions. The discomfort can be a motivator. It pushes you toward looking for solutions.

Of even more importance, knowing your roadblocks can help you determine if the reasons to stay outweigh the reasons to go. If your roadblocks are so big that you probably should let go of the idea of living abroad, either for the short term or perhaps forever, then isn't it better to know now before you uproot your life?

Remember, not going would be the worst-case scenario. I'm a big believer in finding solutions. In fact, I think you can see by my examples that I had some pretty big roadblocks. For a little while I thought maybe the reasons to stay in Denver were too big. Ecuador was just too far.

And that's when it happened. I realized that Ecuador was too far—for now. Maybe I needed to think about my move in terms of smaller steps. Maybe I could move outside the country, but just not so FAR outside the county. I could get my feet wet as an expat. I could spend time learning the language. And I could get all the benefits of living abroad—the lower cost of living, great healthcare, and the adventure of living in a new country—but I could do it closer to home.

I thought about the situation differently. And because of that, I was able to visualize my life abroad in baby steps. I found a location that was just over the border. Someplace where I could drive my car, with my dog safely tucked into the back seat. It was a place that was just an hour or so from the San Diego airport, so I could get back to my mother quickly, if she needed me. Heck, I could bring her down to visit! That was something I wouldn't have considered with Ecuador. And finally, my sweetie could easily come and visit me regularly—putting less strain on our relationship.

So what can you do about your roadblocks?

Think about how you might lessen the impact or eliminate each of the roadblocks you listed. What would you need to do or have so that this roadblock would no longer be an issue?

Here are a few things you might want to think about:

1. If you thought about a different location, would that solve some of your roadblocks?

2. What if you lived abroad part-time or temporarily?

3. Is there a technological solution? Maybe you could set up Skype cameras for all your grandchildren to keep in touch (or have them set them up themselves as they seem to be way ahead of us with technology).

4. Will the money you save on cost of living help you to overcome any of your roadblocks?

5. Maybe you could find countries that have lower cultural, political or language barriers for you. For example: They speak English in Ireland, Belize, and the island of Roatan in Honduras. They use the U.S. dollar in Panama and Ecuador.

6. Would talking to expats in the country you are considering help to ease your fears?

7. Is there a way to take your business or job abroad? With the internet and a good phone line, more and more people are doing just that!

The answers may not come to you all at once. Sometimes you have to leave them there. You have to let them make you uncomfortable. That will get the wheels in your mind churning to find a solution so that you move away from your discomfort.

So take a moment and write down a few ideas you have about how you might overcome those pesky roadblocks.

_____

_____

_____

_____

_____

_____

_____

_____

_____

_____

Expats

As one of the suggestions for overcoming your roadblocks, I suggest that you talk about it with expats who are already living in the country where you want to move. This is an important part of any process of moving abroad, so I want to go over it in more detail.

One of the very best things you can do for yourself is to make friends with the people who have already walked the path that you are about to walk. They can help you overcome so many roadblocks, because they've overcome them too! If you wonder how you are going to stay in touch with your family, they can tell you how they do it. If you want to know if there are foods that match your dietary requirements, they can tell you what stores will have them and what problems you may experience.

The Appendix at the back of the book provides links that will help you find answers to a lot of your questions, including how to connect with expats. They are a wealth of information about the location where they are living and you will do yourself a favor to connect with them. You'll find that the answers they give to some of your questions will help you overcome your roadblocks and give you a realistic image of what you'll be facing in terms of relocating and what difficulties you'll bring with you.

One of the reasons I formed my company, EnjoyLivingInternationally.com, was because I wanted to help people learn from my experience of moving abroad. I wanted to provide them with information and resources. You will find that a lot of expats are just like me. They love helping newbies find their way to this wonderful retirement lifestyle.

So before you throw in the towel, be sure to connect with expats in other countries and see if they overcame the same kinds of problems that you are currently facing.

The Bottom Line...

Whatever is holding you back from making this change in your life can be addressed. And once it is, you will know so much more clearly if moving abroad is right for you at this particular time...or if you need to do a few more things or switch some things around so that you can resolve your roadblocks.

And now, I want you to take a minute and do something for me.

Take a moment and pat yourself on the back. This is not an easy chapter. I made you look at the very things you probably didn't want to look at. But answer me honestly, did it help? Maybe just a little bit? A lot?

Did your mind start spinning, coming up with ways to make your dreams more important than your roadblocks? Maybe you surprised yourself with some new ideas or interesting solutions?

I hope you keep at it! Keep looking at ways to overcome those roadblocks. Think about them differently. Most of all connect with those expats so that you can benefit from their experience.

You can keep your dreams alive and move into them if you don't shy away from whatever roadblocks you have and come up with creative ways to change them into positives.

So take a deep breath and let's move on.

THIS MUST BE THE PLACE

CHAPTER SEVEN: PICK YOUR LOCATION

THINK BACK TO ALL THE WORK YOU HAVE DONE SO FAR. YOU HAVE accomplished a lot that is taking you closer to your dream of living abroad. You now know your Top 5 Life Priorities and your Top 5 Daily Priorities (both from Chapter 1). You understand the many options you have for how you might choose to live abroad (from Chapter 2). You've worked out your financial considerations (Chapter 3). You've gotten clear about your preferences around language in your new country (Chapter 4). AND, you've seriously considered your ability to embrace change, which is an important aspect for absolutely everyone who moves abroad (Chapter 5). Plus, you have sorted through the various obstacles that have shown up and figured out how to deal with them (Chapter 6).

You've done GREAT!

And now you get to do what you've wanted to do since you bought this book – look at where you want to go.

All the work you did in the first six chapters have provided you a solid platform so you can move into one of the most exciting parts of the process – finding that specific place that fits your needs! So let's begin right now.

What places jump into your mind as possibilities for where you might move? You can go really high level and list only countries. Sometimes, it might be that you've just always wanted to live in France and are very unclear of where. So you can just enter France. However, if you have specific cities, towns, or villages of interest, that's even better.

Use the *Where To Go* chart below and list between three and seven locations you've had on your radar. If you have more, there's room for up to ten. Be as complete as possible in the first two columns. Maybe you have two or more locations within the same country. Each is entered separately. The idea here is for you to capture your wish list of places you'd like to live.

Don't do anything with the rest of the columns at this point.

Country	Region, City/Town, etc.	Top 5 Life Priorities	Top 5 Daily Needs	Learn a New Language	Financial Needs	Adapt to Change	Total

Now the fun begins!

It's time to complete the third column, "Top Five Life Priorities".

First, pull out your Top Five Life Priorities from Chapter 1. Using a scale from 1-5, with 1 meaning it doesn't support any of your Top 5 Priorities and 5 meaning it supports all of them, rate each location as to how well it meets those priorities. Remember, column three is only about your Top Five Life Priorities.

And yes, you just might have to do some research in order to rate each location. For example, if you have a very strong need for a particular religious community, and it is one of your Top Five Life Priorities, then you need to make sure that it is available. If, in retrospect, it doesn't really matter that much, then it shouldn't be on your Top Five list in the first place.

You need to be very honest with yourself here and not fudge the results because you've just 'always' wanted to live in a certain place that's on that list. If it's truly the right place for you, it will stand up to your serious evaluation. Believe me, if I'd overrated where I was absolutely sure I should go, I would have been miserable.

Going Deeper

Now that you've identified a few locations that meet your most basic needs and desires, your Top Five Life Priorities, let's go deeper.

It's time to look at your Top Five Daily Needs list. Sometimes a place that meets your most important priorities falls short when you look at what you need on a day-to-day basis. That certainly happened to me. I was sure I'd go live in France because it met all my Top Five Life Priorities. Then I looked at the cost of living and decided it was time to reconsider.

What you will do now is the same thing you did to rate your Top Five Life Priorities. You will use the same scale of 1-5, where 5 means the location meets all your Daily Needs and 1 means it meets none of them. In the fourth column of the chart above, rate each location on how well it will support what you will need to make your day-to-day life as stress-free as possible, with a large helping of fun included.

Most likely you will need to do some deeper research into the area. The Internet has lots of information. One of your first Internet searches should be for expat communities within the region you are considering. Expat communities are invaluable for information from people who have done what you are planning to do. Another valuable resource will be the expat blogs about living in that area. You can also visit your local library and ask the reference librarian if there are any books that might give you the information you want. A fun way to research is to visit each of your locations of interest to see if what you are learning is accurate. (I know visiting your dream locations will be a hardship, but someone's got to do it. And yes, I also understand making such visits is expensive. However, if you can afford it, it's absolutely the best way to do your research. Boots on the ground always trumps the web.)

What you've done to this point with the chart is to look at each location you listed and compared it to your Top Five Life Priorities and your Top Five Daily Needs. Do you feel that you've done enough research and digging that you have rated them correctly in terms of what you want? This is truly where the rubber meets the road. If you rate a location high because it's always been on your dream list but yet it doesn't really meet your Life Priorities or your Daily Needs, you have just set yourself up for serious disappointment. And once you start down that road, you will only keep piling more onto an upcoming mistake. It will end up costing you money, time, energy, and could, quite possibly, kill your dream. Remember to be very honest with yourself. You aren't doing this chart for someone else; you are doing it for you, so that you will live your life as you want to today. It is not based on a preference you made months to years ago before you actually knew what you wanted that life to be.

Once you've double-checked yourself on how you rated each location in columns three and four, you are ready to move on to columns five through seven.

You've already taken a good look at your preferences around language. Using the same rating system as you did for columns three and four, rate each location on how it will allow you to live there and fulfill your determination about whether or not you learn a new language. Write your rating (1-5) for each location.

Now, on to column six. Finances remain a very critical piece of the puzzle for everyone, even if money isn't a real issue. We always want to make good financial decisions and where we live is certainly one area that we all consider. You did a lot of work in Chapter 3 about your financial needs, so that you would be able to evaluate potential possibilities using those needs as part of your criteria.

Take another look at what you came up with in Chapter 3 for your financial needs. Using that information, again rate each location using the 1-5 system.

I bet you are starting to see some definitive results.

But before you start playing with your results, it's important that you complete the chart... do one other exercise and plan a future activity.

This might be the hardest rating to do – or the easiest, depending on what you learned about yourself in Chapter 4. The seventh column is where you will rate how well you believe you will be able to embrace the change you will face in each location. Again, it is important that you be honest with yourself. If you wish it didn't bother you that there is no recycling program and yet it really bothers you deeply, then that is not a change you may be able to embrace. It will depend on how deeply you feel about it, how much you want to become involved in making a difference around that particular behavior, and/or how much experience you have had with facing that in other traveling you have done. Many times such a challenge to you requires understanding the priorities of the people who live where you are considering. For example, there are many places where meeting the basics of food, shelter, and clothing, plus education for children, means that recycling is way down the list. Other times it's more a case of not knowing how to put such a program together.

Carefully think about each location and, once again, rate each in terms of how well you believe you can embrace the change that will be required if you live there.

You have now completed all but one column of the *Where To Go* chart and can see how places that you are interested in living rank against each other.

So what are the other two pieces for you to do right now?

First, go back to the work you did in Chapter 1. Before you selected your Top Five Life Priorities and Top Five Daily Needs, you made a Big List of possibilities for each one. Take a quick look and see if anything on either of those lists changes anything you think about the results you have recorded on your Where To Go chart.

One way to do that is to record below any of the items that seem to really jump out at you. You can then do some additional research in order to feel confident in your move.

_____

_____

_____

_____

_____

_____

_____

_____

_____

_____

Once you've done that, if anything changes your thinking about one or more of your locations, update your ranking for Column 3 and/or Column 4. Be sure to make a notation as to why you made the change, e.g., Life Big List #8 or Daily Big List #12. Down the line you may want to revisit your Where To Go rankings and this will help you understand them.

Now that you've identified your most basic wants and needs, found a location that can meet them, and researched all the other ways it can meet your desires (language, finances, change), you are ready to take the final step before your move.

Well, almost.

First, go back to the *Where To Go* chart and write the totals for each location. Just add up what you ranked the first location in each of the columns and put that in the last column to the right of the location. Do that for each location you evaluated. You can now easily see how each location compares to the others.

Were there any surprises? I certainly had some. As I've mentioned before, I thought I'd live in France and that became evident it would be a mistake. Then I was sure I'd go to Cuenca, Ecuador and even started putting the pieces in place to do that. But, fortunately, through this process that you've just gone through, I realized my mistake before I actually took the plunge. And now I'm living someplace I didn't even have on my radar before I began looking at all the issues you addressed in the first four chapters. Rosarito, Baja California, Mexico. Who would have thought I'd live here? Not me, but I do and I'm very happy with how everything is turning out.

Okay, now on to the last activity in this chapter. And this one can be SO fun!

You know the location that has come up as the place that will best meet what you want for your retirement abroad. So why not go there?

Pick a time when you can be gone for at least four to six weeks. Rent a place that is in a location that will be right for you. You've certainly done enough work to have an idea about that. And don't forget that expats are a fantastic resource for picking a place to rent.

The cool thing about renting for such a short period of time is that you can explore the area and decide on a different location for a longer visit. That worked really well for me as I started with a condo on the eleventh floor of a development south of Rosarito. I fell in love with the city and decided to stay for another six months so I moved within the same complex to what is called a villa (don't let the name impress you, it was a 2BR, 2BA attached house, they just needed to differentiate it from the condos, and villa sounds so cool). What I learned living there is that I still loved Rosarito and wanted to live in the heart of the city, so I could walk most places I wanted to go. The complex where I had been living in the condo and the villa were just far enough on the outskirts that I had to drive everywhere. Now I live in a delightful community with a grocery store one block away, lots of restaurants within walking distance, and only seven walking minutes from the beach, unless I stop and talk with my neighbors or am invited in for coffee, which happens pretty much every day.

So take the time to rent a place in your number one spot. Spend the time living like a local. By the end of that time, you'll know one of three things:

» This is the right place for you.
» Moving isn't for you. You just want extended trips outside your home country.
» You must have been crazy to have had such a wacky idea.

What you learn will make your life much easier. You'll move with the confidence of knowing that you have thoroughly researched your choice and found it to be the best option for you.

FAMILY AFFAIR

CHAPTER EIGHT: STAYING CONNECTED

Just so you know... your friends and relatives are terrified that you are leaving. Oh, they'll act excited.

Yea! Congratulations! We are so excited for you!

Don't believe it.

Whether it's abandonment issues or your mom's need for control, what they really want is to keep you safe, at home, with them. So it's no surprise that one of the most emotionally difficult parts of moving out of country is that you will be leaving behind your friends and family.

That's why it's so important for you to be able to offer reassurance to the people closest to you that you will not lose touch. Having a plan for communicating and staying connected can help your friends and relatives feel more confident about your decision and your move. It will also help them feel less abandoned and more loved and supported.

Your plan for staying connected should do three things: set a list of relationship priorities, organize timetables and methods of connecting, and create a clear emergency plan to handle problems.

#1 Relationship Priorities

Sometimes it is hard to balance all our different commitments. I went to grad school at the same time I was working full time for a biotech company. It took about three months before I realized that I just didn't have the time and energy to continue staying in touch with absolutely everyone in my life -- all the friends I spent time with, from those I was really close with to those I enjoyed more superficially. And, of course, there was my family, some who lived nearby and others who lived in other states.

So I made a list of those people who were most important to me. And then I made a commitment to myself to connect with them regularly and put my other relationships on the back burner. When I finished my master's degree, those same friends threw me a party. None of them knew I had a list, only that I had made the effort to stay connected.

This section will help you identify the people with whom you need or want to stay in regular contact. Remember that your priorities may change when you are living in a different country. It may be that at home you contacted your friends more often than your family, but when you move abroad, your family may be more worried and require more contact.

Using the chart below, make your own list of those who are important enough to you that you want to maintain connection regularly. Enter their names in the column marked Name. Once you've done that, consider with what frequency (monthly, weekly, daily, etc.) you want to stay in touch and enter that information in the second column, Frequency of Connection. For now, don't complete the third column (How Will Stay in Touch).

Name	Frequency of Connection	How Will Stay in Touch

If the list seems overwhelming and you are wondering how you will keep up with them, don't worry. We will be giving you strategies for staying connected in ways that will still let you focus most of your time on your new life.

The good news is that the Internet provides us with many more opportunities to stay in touch, even if we live half a world away. In the next section, you will put together strategies to help you manage your time and still keep those important connections alive.

What do they need?

Sometimes this is the hardest part. It's necessary, before you leave, to figure out what your family and friends need from you; what you need from them is equally important. There are several options for keeping in contact, but all parties should be clear on how frequently you'll be able to guarantee contact, whether they should expect hour long phone calls or lengthy emails. What if you both want to cover everything the other has missed? A call to do this could get very lengthy, especially in the beginning when you're experiencing all new things, and your family wants to tell you about all the people still asking about you and who wants to contact you. Not to mention the latest gossip in the neighborhood, family, church, you name it.

And I'm not saying this is not important stuff to your family. My mom's in her 90's and she wants to talk with me every day. She's important to me and so I make time to talk with her. I've been clear that our calls will be fairly short, 10-20 minutes at the most, and that I'll talk with her every day. What I've done is put the responsibility on her to call me. There are a couple reasons for that. One is that by having her call me, I know that she is still capable of certain motor skills. The other is that I can pay attention to any subtle clues in her conversation that tell me she needs more onsite attention than she is receiving. Since my sisters are talking with her as well, we can chat together at least every month and compare notes. And if any of us become concerned about what we believe we're hearing from her, we can get in touch with each other right away.

This allows me to be relaxed about my mom and she can be relaxed about me…because we are talking as often as she needs it.

What you'll also notice is that my sisters and I have agreed that a monthly phone call is okay for now. That can change for any number of reasons and we'll adjust as needed.

This process is not always easy. It's all about emotional difficulties and translating them into systems that are doable. Remember to share optimism with your loved ones when you do speak, and they will share optimism back.

And now, let's go over two other concerns for keeping in contact.

Time Zones

This one is a doozy. Depending on where you are abroad, your clock is not always going to neatly line up with the time zone of the ones you're trying to keep in contact with. This is a key point to discuss when you're making your plan of how to communicate with each other. In some cases, it's much easier to send emails that can be read on each other's personal time, than trying to schedule a call to accommodate everyone's schedule. Maybe consider setting up a standing phone call, but cushion around that phone call with weekly emails, or short messages utilizing social media. It won't benefit either of you if you make time to chat in the middle of your day, just to be pushed to voicemail because your loved one is sleeping. Time zones can be a huge frustration, making it all the better to map out ahead of time.

Boundaries

Boundaries are crucial when you're setting up communication systems with your friends and family back home. Emails are acceptable to receive any time of the day because they sit quietly in your inbox until you're ready to read them. But what about family that repeatedly calls and gets frustrated when you don't answer, or who aren't content with how much time you have to give? These are boundaries that everyone needs to disclose and respect. Reassure your family that you're going to do your best to stay engaged in all of their lives and keep them in the loop with yours.

The key is to create a plan for each person so that s/he can understand and agree on it. By following it, no one winds up upset, or panicking. And don't worry, most of the plans will be identical to each other. You just want each person to understand their importance to you and that you are taking the time to set up a communication plan that will meet both of your needs.

One very critical piece of setting boundaries is to clearly define what an emergency is. One person's emergency is another's "okay, need to take care of that in the next week". So if everyone understands what constitutes an emergency, then no one is crying "wolf" and emergencies are dealt with as they should be.

The key is to get it in writing and everyone has a copy. Your plan will include:

» Emergency contacts
» Emergency plan specific to each individual
» Definitions of emergencies
» How each type of emergency will be dealt with
  » Timeframe for first contact
  » Will you return and, if so…
  » Will you return immediately?
  » Will you return within a week (and be sure you are returning for legitimate reasons, not just to soothe another's angst)?
  » Will you want someone to come to you?

> » Is there a pool of money that will be used by you to return or by anyone who comes to your aid or will each person be responsible for his or her own expenses?

And finally, be sure to consider events that are not emergencies, such as graduations, weddings, reunions, specific holidays, etc. Will you return for those? If not, you need to set the expectations up front. If you will, be sure to set aside funds to allow you to do that and then let people know you intend to be there. This will alleviate a lot of concern. And over time you may find that you don't return as often and, as long as you keep your friends and family in the loop, they will come to accept it.

#2 Time Tables & Methods for Connecting

Now that you have your list, let's discuss several options for how to stay connected with minimal time commitment. And please don't think that "minimal time commitment" means you are displaying a lack of caring for these important people in your life. By planning the most efficient way to stay in touch with each of them, you will make it easier to stay connected, which is your goal. So don't lose sight of that and focus on what will work best for you.

Low Cost & Low Maintenance

The Internet offers a number of ways for you to connect with your friends and family, without eating up a lot of time. Here are some options that can be a lifesaver:

Blogging

Top Free Blogging Sites:

» www.Wordpress.com

» www.blogger.com

» www.blogspot.com

Blogging about your experience is a great way to keep your friends and family in the loop and actively participating in your life. Don't like to write? You can do a photo and audio blog or a video blog that will show them all the interesting things you are experiencing. This approach has several benefits. First, you can reach all your friends and family through one blog post, instead of contacting them individually. Second, many of your closest family and friends will feel more at ease when they can see how you are doing and hear the joy in your voice. Finally, it has the added benefit of helping them to understand how busy you are and why you may not always be available to write private emails or talk by phone.

Starting your blog before you go can help your friends and family get prepared and excited about your trip. It can ease their worries about losing touch or about your choice of living out-of-country. Write about:

What you're doing to prepare yourself.

» What kind of decisions are you needing to make and how you are researching the answers.

» Where you have decided to go and information that will help people understand why you've chosen that particular place.

» Pictures, information and fun stuff about your new location, and what you plan to do when you get there.

After you're there:

» Show videos, pictures, and tell stories about what it was like arriving in that country.

» Post pictures of your new home and surrounding area. Talk about your neighbors and any new friends you meet.

» Share your meetings with other expats.

» Explain joys and tribulations of food in a foreign land.

» Write about your biggest challenges and how you met them.

» Make them jealous with all your adventures and fun.

» Touch upon how living in your new place makes a difference in your life.

Make sure to post lots of photos and videos that show your new life. Be sure to include brief explanations, especially for those unusual pictures showing cultural differences or activities your friends may not understand.

Facebook

If you are traveling abroad, Facebook can be your best friend for keeping in touch. In less than fifteen minutes per day, you can stay up to date on what your friends and family are doing and help them do the same with you. Upload pictures and videos of your experience. Post daily comments and check for comments from your friends. This is a great alternative to maintaining a blog. Plus, if you have a smart phone, with local phone service, you can check updates and post comments from wherever you are.

Recently, a friend of mine had a nineteen year-old daughter who was traveling through Italy on a student program. They used Facebook to connect each day. So when her daughter didn't check in at her normal time, she knew something was wrong. She was quickly able to contact the student program and learned that her daughter had fallen ill. She used Facebook to stay in touch hourly with the people caring for her daughter and relay the news out to their extended family. It made a scary situation feel more manageable -- especially when her daughter posted a picture of herself giving thumbs up after she recovered.

Twitter

For Tweeps who love to use the blue bird, Twitter can be a great way to keep in touch with friends. In short 140 character bursts, you can send out bits of your daily life to a large number of your friends. Set up a private Twitter account for your trip, and then invite your friends to join. Of course, the only drawback is that some of your friends might not be

Twitter-users. It's up to you to decide if this Internet service will work for your circle of friends or if they'd be more comfortable with one of the other options.

Viber

Viber is a great app for either your phone or desktop. It lets you send free messages, as well as make free calls to other Viber users, on any device and network in any country. It boasts free texting, calling, photo messaging, and location sharing with Viber users. No registration or invitations are required and it's so easy to load your contact list into.

Medium Cost or Time Maintenance
Email

While completely free, email can be somewhat time consuming. I mean, do you really want to spend hours answering emails when you could be hiking the rain forest or shopping in that quaint village? Here's how to manage it:

» Tell people that you will only be monitoring a specific email address while you are away.

» Only give out that email address to a few people -- those on your short list (you will be defining that list below).

» Provide your extended network of friends with an alternate means of communicating with you -- such as Facebook, your blog, or Twitter account.

Follow these three tips and—voila! You'll have a more organized and easier to manage system for connecting through email.

Skype

Phoning can be expensive and time consuming. VoIP (voice over Internet protocol) calling systems can help with the cost. However, you will need to come up with a plan for managing your time.

There are quite a few VoIP companies that can help you set up low cost international calling. Skype is one of them, and what makes them a good choice is that they offer several of their services, including video calling, for **free**. You need to be aware that the free calling exists only for Skype to Skype calls, so you and your family and friends will want to sign up for the free Skype service before you leave.

Skype's video option will require that both your computer and the computer you are calling have webcams. If not, you can purchase a videophone from Skype or on the web. This is a great way to stay in touch with friends and family back home, without breaking the bank. Our suggestion is to set up a regular time, such as every Sunday or one day each month to call and catch up with your favorite people back home. You can alternate your calling circle each time or just give your Skype number out to a handful of people.

MagicJack

This is another option available for low cost long distance calling via the Internet. With this device, you can hook up a phone to your computer and use the computer's Internet to make phone calls. This option is not free, but it is much less expensive than a standard phone line. Many of my friends use this service.

Vonage

This VoIP also charges and is more expensive than MagicJack. This is what I use and can make unlimited calls back to the U.S. I can also make calls to other countries by checking the Vonage web site to see if calling that country is in my plan.

Keep in mind that any service that is used over the internet, be it Skype, MagicJack, Vonage, or anything else, is dependent on the reliability of your internet connection. If you have a good Internet service, your calls should be fine. If it's spotty, you may have to deal with dropped calls.

Just don't make yourself crazy over it. You'll get into your rhythm once you get set up.

High Cost & High Maintenance
Visits and Visiting

If you are planning to be gone for an extended period of time, there will be moments when even a videophone won't be enough. Plan for trips home or for your loved ones to visit you. Make sure you don't do it too early in your time abroad or you might establish an expensive habit. Homesickness happens. Try to ride out the early waves by keeping yourself busy exploring your new home. If you are really homesick early on, then schedule a trip for six months down the road. That way you will have it as a goal to keep your mind happy and you won't be tempted to go home too early. Also, if your friends and family are clamoring to visit you, then set boundaries. Let them know that you'll be more available for their visits in a few months or that you can only host them for a certain number of days. You have a new life to live so keeping visits within a manageable time-frame will help you to connect more deeply to your new world.

Putting your Plan Together

Now that you have a better understanding of some of your options for connecting with loved ones. Using what you've learned over the last several pages about various methods for staying in contact, pick those options you believe will work best for each person. For some, you may find that connecting with them works best through comments on your blog or on Facebook, or maybe with an email or phone call once every few months. For others, more attention may be necessary. Making this list will help you manage your time and make sure the important people in your life still feel important while you are away.

Keep in mind that some of the people you want to stay connected with will need to have some help getting set up with whatever method you chose to use with them.

For example, your grandmother may need help getting Skype set up and will have to be trained on how to use it. Or maybe she isn't comfortable with computers so you set a schedule to talk with her when another family member can be with her and set up a Skype video call with you.

What's important is that you let each person know how important they are to you and how you will stay in touch. This goes a very long way to helping people accept your new adventure and to realize that, in a way, you are taking them along.

GOT TO BE REAL

CHAPTER NINE: LOGISTICS

TRAFFIC CONTROL POINT

TRAFFIC CONTROL POINT

Moving to a foreign country is often a wild ride and there is only one thing you can count on—very little will go as expected. So take a deep breath. Embracing the changes and preparing for them will only help your transition go smoothly. Fortunately, there are a few areas where you can anticipate obstacles and greet them with open arms—because you are prepared.

Of course, it all depends on the ultimate question – are you *willing* to embrace change?

We can give you all the tips and tricks available, but if you're set on a certain experience and have no wiggle room, the transition will probably be anything but smooth.

This chapter will cover the most important factors for you to keep in mind as you consider all the changes you'll likely face.

Taking Things for Granted

The easiest mistake to make is to take the comforts of home for granted. Start now considering all the things that you love about where you live and the ease with which they come to you. Now, take a deep breath and start to say your good-byes. The most common aspects that are taken for granted are:

» Goods

» Services

» Family

» Friends

The first step to take when appreciating the differences you'll face in your new location is to determine what you **have** to have. It'll be a tradeoff between the amenities and sacrifices. Maybe you'll get a great deal on a beautiful apartment, in a beautiful location…but you won't have central air conditioning or heating. American architecture offers many comforts that we don't really consider when we're moving somewhere else. Consider weather-stripping; there is usually none in other locations. Restaurant etiquette will be different, driving expectations are different. For example, in some countries, the turn signal is meant to indicate to the following car what they should actually do, rather than what the driver is about to do on the road. One comparison I make between driving in Mexico and driving in the US is that, in the US, it's all about the rules. In Mexico it's all about the dance. I actually enjoy driving in Mexico but I had to first embrace the difference.

The Legal Issues

Government and legal bureaucracy is a hassle no matter where you go. Don't give up! Instead, plan on researching issues at least three or four months in advance and you will prevent frustrated explosions and frequent cursing (out loud or maybe just inside your head).

Here's a list of legal issues that you'll want to research:

» Vaccines for you and your pet & potential quarantines for pets.

» Required documents such as passport, visa, and/or work permits.

» Maximum length of stay under your visa. Rules regarding leaving and returning.

» Your citizenship country's warnings or restrictions.

» Insurance issues

» Residency requirements

» Location and contact information of your local embassy.

- » Local tax laws and the tax laws for your home country in regard to living abroad
- » Local business & employment laws (if you plan to run a business or work)

It's very important that you check out the visa requirements for your new country. What is required can vary greatly from one country to the next. Many countries require visas for extended stays of more than 30 days. The average visa will let you stay in a country for 90 days and sometimes you can get a different visa that will let you stay 180 days. If you plan to stay in a country for longer than the term of a simple visa (three to six months), be sure to research what the requirements are for doing so. If you plan to stay for an extended period of years, you will need to get a residency permit. Each country will have different laws regarding living and working in their country. Be sure to research online or contact that embassy in your own country. They should be able to provide you with information and help you get the paperwork started for a visa or residency status.

When you arrive in a country, you will want to register with your local embassy. This can help you during emergency situations and help your government contact you if there is an evacuation. You will want to bring your passport or other proof of citizenship when registering in person. In addition to the requirements of your new country, there are documents and records that you will need in case of emergency, work issues, visa, or residency issues and more.

Be sure to bring a copy of the following items:

- » Birth and marriage certificates
- » Proof of citizenship: visa, passport, driver's license, voters, and social security cards
- » Medical records and/or vaccination records
- » Medical arrangements or living will

» Pet health information & vaccination records

Having all of these issues worked out before you leave can eliminate headaches once you are in your new country. You will want to keep copies of documents in a safe place, and also leave a copy with someone you trust back home. That way if you lose yours, they can send you the copies.

Once you are in a country, you also want to check on the local equivalents of wills, medical arrangements, and any instructions you have concerning your health and well-being. Do not count on your home country documents being valid for things such as sending your remains home or not using extraordinary measure should you have a heart attack. Be sure you have documents that are valid in your new country.

This is when you may find it in your best interest to locate an in-country lawyer to review everything. Your lawyer can help you make sure that what you want and expect to have happen in given circumstances, will actually occur, or explain to you why your wishes cannot be accommodated. You do not want to wait for surprises when you or your loved ones are at your/their most vulnerable.

Medical

Most countries have some sort of government run healthcare. The good news is that you may not be out of pocket if an emergency situation pops up. However, some of the government run hospitals have long waits and subpar care, and others are as good or better than anything you would get back home.

Be sure to check out the hospitals in your area. In most urban areas there are several to choose from and they offer differing levels of care. Some countries have mixed healthcare offerings of government run and private facilities. Find out which works best for your needs and what you need to do to qualify for their care. In some countries, you pay extra for faster ambulance services. In others, you can get private insurance to cover trips to the private medical facilities.

Also, look into how prescriptions are handled. Many drugs that require prescriptions in the U.S. are over-the-counter in other countries. Check out how much they cost because you will probably find they cost less, sometimes substantially so. One man I met in Cuenca, Ecuador brought all his meds with him to an appointment with a doctor. His only purpose for the appointment was to discuss which medications required prescriptions, which were available in Ecuador, and, if they weren't available, what were the equivalents.

Sanitation & Infrastructure

I hate outhouses, don't you? Well, maybe not for the short term but definitely not as a way of life. Living in a modern nation means that we've come to assume a certain level of infrastructure and sanitation. You expect that your water will come out of the tap when you turn it on and that it will be clean and safe. You expect that your garbage will be picked up each week and the electricity will be there at the flip of a switch. You expect that your banks will be accurate and the customer service friendly.

Though many countries have improved greatly in the past few decades, if you have decided to move to a second or third world nation, then be prepared for the possibility of poor or sporadic utilities and sanitation. We suggest contacting local expats to find out what you can expect. If you are planning to run an Internet business, then find out how reliable the Internet services are and how expensive. If you have a sensitive stomach, research the water and food cleanliness of the area where you plan to live.

A quick story about doing the right research. A friend told me of a relative who had left Ethiopia due to a regime change. His house was confiscated by the government and, after yet another change many years later, he decided to get it back. It took two years and a fair amount of money and he and his family were able to move in. What he'd neglected to research was broadband availability for his Internet based business. Although his family lived in their lovely home, he had to live in Addis Ababa during the week as that was the only way he could run his business.

The key to getting what you expect is research. In some countries the infrastructure is better in some cities than in others. For example: Alexandria, Egypt is a relatively clean city with good street sanitation, whereas Cairo is not able to keep up with the trash of its huge population. Many of it's people are forced to use their backyards or the canals coming off the Nile as a place to dispose of their trash, which in turn causes sanitary problems. Sometimes the infrastructure is unexpectedly good. When I visited Cuenca, Ecuador, the majority of the streets were cleaner than ones I've found in downtown areas of the United States.

Utilities

Don't you just love dealing with utility companies? Imagine how much more fun it will be in a different country. Well, here are some tips on how to prevent the experience from feeling like a root canal gone wrong.

Keep in mind everything that needs to be set up and accomplished. Adjust your time schedule for things to get done. This is one aspect of moving abroad that truly needs to be embraced: it is quite often a very different mindset, with different expectations, when it comes to work in other countries.

Having come from the US, I was used to picking up the phone to set up all utilities and services and being able to get everything well on its way in one day. What I have learned living abroad is that if I want to remain sane (or close to it), handling one thing a day, rather than five, is the best approach, especially if there is a language barrier. Standing in line is a fact of life in many countries and if you load yourself up with a To-Do List that has several items on it, you will become frustrated and make the process much harder on yourself. Learning to "chill" is a great art to develop.

Because here's the thing. If I try to set up all the utilities in one day, first, it won't happen; second, I'll be exhausted and angry; third, I'll have to go through the same type of routine again the next day. Ultimately, it will take just as long to do one utility per day as trying to do as many as possible each day. So give yourself a break and take this as one of your first opportunities to adjust to your new cultural environment.

I suggest you assign yourself one utility, do as much as you can, and then reward yourself with a beverage of choice at a café where you can relax, a pint in a pub, or whatever turns your crank. For me, it's a dish of ice cream and watching the waves roll in.

The most important utilities to remember and prioritize will be:

» Electric/gas – usually different companies
» Landline phone and/or cell phone – usually different companies
» Internet services
» Water
» Trash

When talking with the various personnel at the different utility offices, be as specific in your language as possible. Words that are used back home may not mean the same thing in your new location. *Thing* is a kind of slang. Suggestion: use a more specific word, such as *problem, issue, dilemma,* etc.

Remember, you always have a fallback when arranging your utilities. Contact the expat community and ask if there is anyone who is available for hire to help you set them up. This is particularly helpful when you do not speak the language of the country very well. Plus, they will know where all the offices are, what the options are, and the drill for setting up your service. Additionally, you will learn a great deal about your new community – things that you probably would not have thought to ask until much later and could make a difference now.

Speaking of knowing locations, a friend of mine who was setting up her first phone and Internet service in Mexico asked an expat where the local office was. Because street signs were close to non-existent, she was told to go north on the main boulevard in town, look for the green building on the left whose second floor had burned, and turn left there. The phone company would be half a block down on the left. An hour and a half later she found it. Turns out when a cinderblock building burns, it looks quite different than a framed building. The only clue there had been a second floor was that the roof was completely flat and there was no green paint along the top edge.

Finally, keep in mind that many countries, particularly European countries, have a different electrical system. The voltage might not be safe with your appliances or technology. Consider getting voltage adapters and check out your important equipment, like your computer, to be sure it will be compatible in your new home.

The Move

Are you someone who gleefully loves to pack and unpack? If you are, call me; I could use your help. However, if you are like me (and most people) then you are probably not uber-excited about packing up and moving all your things to your new home.

To make things easier, you'll want to prioritize and create lists of what needs to be done, and when it needs to be done. Giving yourself four to six months prep time to move abroad is truly a gift. It can save you time, money, and migraines. Granted, there are those who make the move in a much shorter time and they are usually people who have been thinking about this for quite some time. They've already thought about what they want to do with their "stuff" even if they haven't actually taken any steps to do it. That makes it much easier to move quickly.

The first part of the move will be the act of getting things ready for the move. Clear out all those things you've been gathering, but never actually use, by giving them to family or friends, having a garage sale, or donating them. Plan your travel and shipping far in advance. Flights and shipping arrangements get more expensive when there are shorter turn around times. You also want plenty of time to get your household organized, your various commitments canceled, and your new living arrangements solidified.

You will want to create a system for listing out all the chores that need to be done and creating a plan for how they'll get done (and in what order). Also, create a timeline and plan for any shipping issues. However you decide to go about it, you want to have an organized system to be sure that your move is smooth and all your items get to where they belong and none are forgotten.

One of the important issues to consider is how much to take. Do you travel light, buy things there, or ship all your things? What you decide depends quite a bit on where you are going and how long you plan to stay. For example, if you are moving to Costa Rica for six months to a year, then shipping all your furniture will be expensive. Many new items can be purchased there for much less expense than shipping. However, say you are moving to southern Italy for at least five years, shipping your furniture would probably save you money.

I have friends living in Ecuador who decided they did not want to ship a lot of stuff and they were also selling their house. They gifted a lot to friends and family, donated as much as possible, tossed a lot, and put only a very small amount into storage at one of their children's homes. So what did they take to Cuenca? Six suitcases. Yep, that was everything they had determined they really needed. And what was even cooler was that they took them as checked luggage when they flew down to move into their rental unit. Yes, they had to pay for the extra baggage but it was seriously cheaper than going through a shipper, plus it was there when they arrived.

Another consideration is your lifestyle. If you plan to move around a lot, it would probably be best to think light. Leave your furnishings behind and rent places that are already furnished. Even if you have to buy a few things that are missing, it's still considerably cheaper than trying to haul a lot of stuff around.

Okay, so let's say you've decided that in your particular situation it will be best to ship your belongings. It is important to note that each country has it's own rules about shipping household goods into their country. You will want to research your country of choice to determine:

» Policies, regulations, and restrictions.

» What items are taxable?

» What documentation might be required?

» Electronics issues - are yours compatible with the local electrical systems?

» Can you import your car or your pet(s)? Are there any associated impound timetables and how about vet records for pets?

Once you understand the country regulations, then you need to sort and organize what you will be taking with you and what will stay behind. Be sure to make a list of the items, where they are stored if leaving behind (and how the box is labeled), and take pictures, especially of anything you are taking with you. This type of documentation can be a blessing if items are lost or broken. You can use them for insurance purposes for the move or even with your local storage company. It also helps when you're trying to remember what you left behind.

Research the shipping company that you choose. Unless it's possible to drive everything to your new residence, you're really looking at three phases of moving -- one to get your things to port, one to ship it to your new country, and one to move everything from the port to your new home. If at all possible, use a single shipper so if anything happens to your shipment, you can contact one company and not have three differ-ent companies claiming it's the other's fault. The shipper you contract with may subcontract but that's their problem, not yours. Also, require that at each point of embarkation and debarkation you have an agent fluent in both your language and the language of workers at that port as well as your new country. As part of your research check with the Better Business Bureau to see how well they are ranked. Research online (using the name of the company and words like "reviews" or "ratings") and be sure to ask the company for references. Another good option is to contact expats where you are moving for their recommendations.

Once you have decided on a company, make sure they have insurance to cover your goods. If they don't cover them adequately, look into a supplemental policy. There are a number of companies that offer shipping insurance, with rates starting as low as $100. Many of these insurance companies will cover your car as well. You want to know how you will be handling insurance *before* you sign a contract to ship your goods. Read carefully what is in the shipping contract and make any changes *before* you sign it. Make sure you have proof, such as a receipt, for any payment you make on the shipping and the insurance. Additionally, you want documented proof that your goods were picked up from the site of origination and that you can track them along the route they will take to your new home.

Also, be sure that you arrive in-country before your household items do. Leaving your things sitting on a dock for days is not only unsafe, but it is a good way to have them get lost. This is where having a good shipping agent can make a huge difference. And why you want an agent who is fluent in both your language and the language of your new country. They can help you identify and coordinate all the parts of your move and help you deal with the customs officials. Working with an agent may also prevent you from paying miscellaneous fees that you shouldn't be charged. If your overseas shipper doesn't have a recommendation for an agent, then find an expat forum online and ask for recommendations.

Having all of these issues worked out before you leave can eliminate headaches once you are in your new country. You will want to keep copies of all documents in a safe place and also leave a copy back home with someone you trust. That way if you lose yours, they can send you the copies.

This is Home, Not a Vacation

When we go on vacation, we have a mind set that is all about fun, relaxing, perhaps a sport (golfing, scuba diving), exploring a rainforest, or visiting museums. It's not about spending more than the minimum of time unpacking and figuring out where things are so you can get on with the vacation.

What you are doing by moving abroad is a very different animal.

This is your new home for the time being. It generally takes about six weeks to feel settled into a new location, and about three months to feel at home in it. Of course you've done your research, you've looked around for what amenities are in your vicinity, but even the most prepared expat can't be expected to have locations and directions memorized first day out the gate. Make it a priority to really turn your new home into a comfortable home. There are small items you can bring to really make the place remind you of the best parts of home. Some of these things can be:

- » Family photos
- » Music that reminds you of your friends and family and puts you in a great mood
- » Small family heirlooms
- » Memory quilts

While you're settling into your new place, venture out to find a local spot to call your own. Some feel at home in a coffee shop with a book or their computer and headphones. Others walk the beach or find a good route to take a daily run or walk. Still others may find a place to have an afternoon ice cream or other snack and just enjoy watching the world go by. Maybe you'll find your 'crowd' at the local sports bar. Remember that the way to begin feeling at home is to connect to others around you and finding a spot you frequent begins that process.

Put in the effort to make this new home yours. The best method is to avoid returning "home" for the first six months or having anyone come visit you in the first three months. Why? Because you need to settle in and taking trips home stops the process. As someone who had to return to Colorado for a family emergency after only being abroad for a few weeks, I found it was very much a starting over process when I returned to my new home. Other expats had warned me this would probably happen and they were right.

As for having visitors from "back home," you'll be much better prepared to entertain them if you've given yourself time to acquaint yourself with your new surroundings. Instead of wondering what you'll do with them, you will already know some fun things to do, restaurants they will enjoy, how to handle the quirky things that come up, and how to make it a very enjoyable experience for them and for yourself. And they will see that you have made a good decision and picked a good spot to live.

Sometimes, try as you might, it doesn't feel like home. Now what?

In this case, it may not be the place that doesn't work for you, it's that you're just in the wrong neighborhood of the right place. It's entirely possible for a certain area to not work for you and yet the location overall is a great match for you. This is where you take the opportunity to explore other neighborhoods, speak to expats in the community, see what other amenities are being offered elsewhere and consider making the move.

Take me, for example. When I first moved to Mexico, I lived for seven months in a gorgeous place that was a couple kilometers south of town. Other than the couch, there wasn't much I didn't like about the place. Except that I had to get in a car and drive anytime I wanted some bananas or to have a lunch out. Plus, the community was mostly transitory and making friends was more difficult. So I looked around and am now living in a wonderful spot in town where I can walk to pay my telephone bill, buy groceries, and have a wealth of restaurants to choose from. And I've met a lot of folks, made quite a few friends, and can walk to many of their homes.

The most important thing for you to remember is that you can make it all happen – from figuring out the legal issues, setting up utilities, to making the actual move. Remember that it doesn't all have to be done in one day or one week or one month. This is a process, just like back home when you move cross-country or around the corner. And you don't have to figure it all out for yourself; there are plenty of expats around to help you.

RUNNING ON EMPTY

CHAPTER TEN: EMERGENCIES & THE UNEXPECTED

DARN IT! NO MATTER HOW MUCH WE PLAN, THE UNEXPECTED WILL come up. Sometimes it's as simple as just being homesick or as complex as a political shift in your new country. These changes can cause us to feel unhappy or insecure in our new home. The key is in planning ahead so we already know what our options are. Whether it's a family emergency, a natural disaster, or disagreements with your neighbors, it is good to have an idea of what your choices are and how to handle the situation.

In this chapter, you will plan what to do when a crisis occurs. You will look at the internal struggles with your decision to move -- things like homesickness, the novelty wearing off, and the daily struggles with language and culture. You will also go over the external factors such as emergencies and unexpected events that can put a wrench in your new life.

#1 Emergencies & Disaster Planning

When we are dreaming of our move to our new country, emergencies are the furthest things from our minds. Yet unfortunate events can happen. Whether it is the death of a family member, a personal health issue, or a local disaster, you will be able to weather it better if you have a strategy in place.

Getting Back Home

One of the best things you can do for peace of mind is to have a way to get to your home country in case of emergencies back home. If you have a death in the family or an unexpected illness, having a backup source of funding for travel expenses will be essential. I recommend a credit card put aside for emergencies only. Having cash on hand is always an option and it's also high risk. If you choose to keep cash, make sure you are careful where you stash it and that you don't mention it to anyone. Bottom line – be sure you have enough funds available for a last-minute flight.

Health Issues

Understanding your new country's healthcare can be the difference between life and death. Put together a listing of local hospitals and clinics. Know how the ambulance service works in your area. Do they have an ambulance service or would it be faster for you to take your sick or injured person to the hospital yourself? How about payment? What kind of charges can you expect and how and when will you be expected to pay? Knowing the answers to these important questions will help you be prepared in the event of a health-related emergency.

Local Disasters or Political Uprisings

It is important to remember that most second and third world nations will not have the infrastructure to support you in case of a national disaster or government emergency. It is in your best interest to take a bit of time and make an emergency plan for you and your family. Once you have it complete, you will have greater peace of mind. Review it regularly with family members so they will be able to act accordingly, meet at an assigned location, and have adequate supplies until help can arrive.

There are three things you will want to have prepared: emergency plan, emergency kit, and an evacuation plan. Here are the essentials for each:

Have an Emergency Plan

Begin by staying aware of any political or environmental concerns there might be, both locally and within the country as a whole. Things such as: Is any part of your new country prone to earthquakes? How about hurricanes or tsunamis? Do protests tend to get out of control? Are there frequent power outages and for how long, on average?

Put in writing a plan for you and your family members, outlining things like: where you will meet if a disaster strikes, how to communicate with family back home, what the contact numbers are for the consulate or embassy, emergency numbers, and a local contact person. Keep all your important documents in a safe place, and, very importantly, have backup photocopies of these items in a different location in case you need them.

Keep a map with your emergency kit that has three evacuation routes out of the country. Try to have options by car, plane, and ship. Outline the meeting points, secondary meeting points, and most direct routes.

Other tips might include:

» Contact your embassy or consulate if an emergency appears imminent. They may have instructions for you.

» Make sure you have a portable radio or access to Internet or television. Keep connected to the local news for information.

» Know the access requirements for nearby countries. Roads, primary and alternate routes, required documentation, etc.

» Know where the police station is located and how to access emergency services and contact police, fire, or ambulance by phone (ex. 911 in the U.S. accesses emergency services).

» Know where nearby hospitals, shelters, and government offices are located. Also, know where your embassy or consulate is, not just the address, but where it is on the map. Going there when you are calm so that you know where it is can help you feel more confident if you need to get there during a crisis.

» Define a primary and secondary meeting place, or staging area, in case family members are apart when emergency strikes. Assign the person at home/nearest home to bring the emergency kit.

» Keep documents & emergency kit handy.

» If you have time, contact people back in your home country to get them ready for what you may need and to tell them your plans for evacuation.

» Money wired or other financial transactions.

» A place to stay, should you need to return to your home country in an emergency.

» Someone to come and help you.

Prepare an extensive emergency kit

Again, you may be in a country that will need to wait for outside help during a crisis. So be prepared with plenty of water and non-perishable food to last for several days for each member of your family. Include other things like: pain-killers, antiseptic, bandages, toilet paper, batteries, candles, flashlights, a radio (preferably solar or crank-powered), a non-electric can opener, and other items necessary to keep you healthy and aware during a crisis. Also, have emergency cash and a credit card with your kit.

Emergency Kit

Emergency questions like: "Where is the doctor?" "How can I get to [my embassy]?" "Where is the shelter?" "Can I get some help?" will be useful if you have them already prepared and can just point to the sentence for people to read.

Item	Location (specific room in house, safe deposit box, safe, etc.)	Check Completed
Universal adapter for electronic devices		
Battery powered phone charger		
Cell phone		
Gas can for car/ generator, filled		
Blankets and/or sleeping bags		
Road maps (if GPS is down)		
Dry/Canned food and water for 5 to 7 days.		
Manual can opener		
1-2 pans to use with stove		
Sterno stove & fuel		

Item	Location (specific room in house, safe deposit box, safe, etc.)	Check Completed
Copies of your passport and other important documents -Print a copy for the kit and also scan to keep them on an online storage or CD.		
Emergency cash (both your home country and local currency) & credit card		
Bag packed with spare clothing & comfortable shoes.		
First Aid kit & Prescription medication		
List of phone numbers & addresses for doctor, hospital, police, pharmacy, plus numbers for those back home		
Language dictionaries for that country and surrounding countries.		
List of specific emergency questions in those languages on a piece of paper.*		
Flashlight, Candles & Batteries		
Transistor radio & more batteries		
Matches (waterproof)		
Backpack		

#2 The Unexpected/Unwelcome

Sometimes problems come up that are unexpected and unwelcome. Here are some tips on how to handle these difficult situations:

Discrimination or Problems with Locals

What do you do when you've moved to a new country only to find that some of the people have misconceptions about your home country or your people? It is important for you to know how to handle situations, so you can be prepared when confronted with this unpleasant experience. Here are a few tips:

Talk It Out

Talk with local expats to learn their experiences and how they overcame these problems.

Be Self-confident

Confidence without arrogance puts a positive face on who you are and what you believe. By this, we mean that if you maintain pride in your appearance and hold your head up high, you will show the prejudiced person that you are not someone to bully. However, being confident does not mean badgering others about your beliefs or demanding that they respect you. That kind of behavior will be construed as aggressive and can lead to further problems.

Be Mindful of Location

Determine if there are locations in the city or country you have chosen that are more accepting. If so, you will want to live and socialize more in these areas and avoid the places with higher levels of bias.

Cultural Behavior

Find out what the appropriate levels of eye contact and personal space are for your new country, such as touching, gestures, or even laughter. You don't want to make a problem worse by not knowing proper body language or etiquette.

Changing Minds

Remember that discrimination comes from ignorance and fear. If you are dealing with low levels of prejudice in your neighbors, over time the regular contact and proper behavior on your part will go a long way toward changing attitudes.

Sometimes it is hard to avoid the most prejudiced of a culture. If you have a run-in or feel that you are in danger, know your rights and contact the authorities. Find local organizations that help to minimize discrimination and ask them for help in working with the people in your neighborhood, schools, or place of employment.

We cannot always avoid unpleasantness or mayhem in the world, but if we are prepared to handle them, then we can get through them more quickly and with a better result. We hope that this chapter has helped you to be more aware of the potential pitfalls and has provided you with the means for overcoming these challenges and creating a more healthy and happy life for yourself.

Remember it's important to plan for the unexpected, while also living fully in the present.

#3 Additional Preparation

Here are a few other steps we encourage you to take:

Government Registration

Register with the embassy for your home country and be sure to keep that information updated if you move. This could be essential in an emergency, as your government may try to contact you to provide you with directions on what to do and where to go.

For U.S. citizens, you can register online:

https://step.state.gov/step/

For Canadian citizens:

http://travel.gc.ca/travelling/registration

Emergency Funds or Power of Attorney

Before you leave your home country, create an account or give Power of Attorney to a person you trust to take action on your behalf and in a manner that follows what you want done. Provide this person with access to funds, health benefits, life insurance, etc. This person can send you funds if you are robbed, if you have a financial catastrophe, or if for some reason, you cannot access your local funds. If an accident leaves you incapacitated, this person can help make decisions on your behalf. It will also give your relatives the means to handle any financial issues in the case of your death.

Emergency Contact Instructions

Make sure that family and friends have a way to get in contact with you in case of emergency. Provide key people with your local phone and address, contact information for the local embassy or consulate, and/or a local neighbor or friend.

Disability or Death - Illness or injury can happen anywhere. Be sure to have documentation on what you want to happen. Do you want your body returned to your home country or will funeral and burial occur in your new country? Have a Will and a Living Will. Make sure there are copies with you and with your trusted individual back home.

None of us want to think about the scary stuff. The point is that if we do, and create ways to deal with a variety of possibilities that could occur, our ability to manage in a crisis is substantially increased.

And then we can relax and enjoy our new home and the adventure of living abroad.

I AM WOMAN

CHAPTER ELEVEN: DIFFERENT CONCERNS

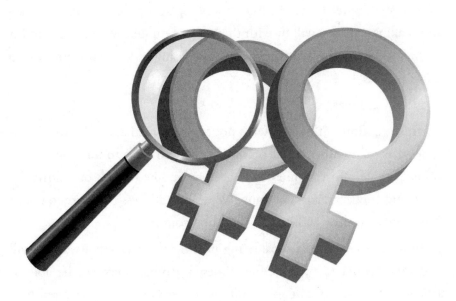

THERE ARE MANY PEOPLE WHO LOOK AT A SINGLE WOMAN WHO CHOOSES to live abroad as someone who is putting herself in harm's way.

A risk-taker.

A daredevil.

I knew that retiring abroad for a woman would have its own challenges and also that the rewards would be amazing opportunities.

Yes, it's true that when moving abroad, women have concerns that a man generally wouldn't consider. Some are obvious, such as safety. Others are more subtle, like making sure that there is a social network of other women she can relate to. Another is looking at the community of expats and making sure she will fit with them based on her own values. In this chapter we are going to cover the issues relating to women who want to move abroad.

However, I want to be clear.

The intention of this chapter is not to set women apart. It's to address issues that many other books on moving abroad seem to leave out. These are issues that affect women and the way we like to live, our particular needs and concerns, and the things we need to address that pertain to our safety and our place within a new cultural context.

And any man who is considering moving abroad with a woman will find this chapter helpful. Often times, a woman may not be able to articulate how important something is to her and what is covered here explains many of those issues.

This chapter seeks to clarify women's needs to help make wise decisions about locations for moving abroad and how to make her move. Sometimes, locations that fit all her other needs such as cost of living, local amenities, or weather will ultimately not meet her needs because the culture does not support women as individuals. If a location requires that women wear particular clothing or are uncomfortable with women acting on their own behalf, then it's important to consider whether that location is the right one.

Even after choosing a location, there are considerations of culture that can affect one's relationship with others within that culture. For example, is it considered taboo for a woman to be out to lunch with a male friend if that friend is married?

Here are a few items that this chapter will examine about being a woman living abroad:

» Family Concerns

» Cultural Expectations

» Lifestyle, Dating & Social Support

» Health & Wellness

» Safety

Each of these areas can make an impact on a woman's life abroad. Let's take a look at how each of them can affect her location choice and how she will relate to others in her new life.

Family Concerns

When women move abroad there seems to be one very important issue that impacts them more than men. They worry about the family they are leaving behind. For some, it is an elderly parent or a sibling. For others, it is their children and grandchildren.

Some of these concerns have been made easier by modern technology. No matter where you are in the world, there is usually a way to access the

Internet. As we mentioned in Chapter 8, you can now use Skype, Facebook, MagicJack and a host of online tools to stay connected with friends and family back home.

But for those with family who are elderly or have health issues, many women feel the tug to be a caretaker for that person. This requires a bit more planning, but a woman set on being a happy expat can organize life for her family member that will put her mind at ease. Again, I don't want it to appear that men don't have these same challenges. They do. It's just that they tend to look more at how they can provide financial assistance, whereas women tend towards the hands-on assistance.

One way of doing this is by sitting down with other members of the family to plan out the care of this family member. That way the burden is not just on one person. All the members can work through a plan on housing, caretaking, and emergency situations. That allows a woman's feet to wander about the world and still be committed to a defined level of help.

It may be through daily phone calls, compensation of the help, and perhaps occasionally taking the family member into her home abroad to give other family members a break. Some people even come to realize that they can care for an aging parent better while in a foreign country. They simply bring them along and, once there, they can afford to hire in-home care and nursing.

Another consideration, if you want to be sure that you can connect with family members, is to choose a location that has an airport that provides easy access to and from the locations you are most likely to visit or have family visit you from. What is especially great is if there are daily (or multiple times per day) flights back to your home country—even better if they have direct flights to a city close to your family.

For women who hope for a more adventurous life abroad, it may mean creating a home base near a city with a major airport and then exploring out from that home base. Sometimes it takes a balance between what we want and our need to stay connected with those we love. But with a little planning and thought, it can be done.

I'm a great example. My mother is in her 90s. I knew that my dream of living in Cuenca, Ecuador would mean I'd have a difficult time getting back to her in case of an emergency. Plus, she had reached an age where my sisters and I agreed that living alone could be dangerous for her. We had a full family discussion and created a plan. In the end, my mother is now well taken care of and each member of my family is happy with the plan. However, I still felt that I needed to be closer to home. So instead of moving to Cuenca, I've chosen a much closer location in Baja, Mexico. That way, I can get to my mother in a matter of hours. Plus, I bring her to visit me and we enjoy spending time together, while my sister who is providing live-in support for our mom gets a much-needed break. I'm still living abroad and enjoying a low cost of living. I'm learning Spanish. And I'm preparing for the day when I will, indeed, move to Cuenca.

Cultural Expectations

The world over, women have a variety of roles—some with more freedoms and equality and some with less. Some cultures have sexism that is fairly subtle while in others it's more overt. It's important to understand the levels and how pervasive these attitudes are. The question every woman needs to ask is if she is willing to live with them day after day.

For example: A friend of mine was in Italy with her mother when her mother experienced a medical emergency. They spent most of the day in the emergency room of a hospital in Rome.

The first thing my friend noticed was that the translator would translate questions from the doctor to her and then her answers. But if the doctor had any additional information about her mother's situation, he would tell the translator and the translator would just nod and keep the information to himself. My friend would consistently have to prod the man into telling her what the doctor thought about the situation. The translator would brush it off by saying they would run tests, but not answer what the tests were for. Several times she had questions for the doctor about her mother's condition, but the doctor acted as if it wasn't important that she understand the situation. It was only important that he and the male translator understood.

It wasn't until she had her mother back on her cruise ship that the ship's doctor, who was Norwegian, was willing to tell her that her mother had gone into a diabetic shock.

The Italian men obviously lived in a world where only men need to know the important information. Even things like lifesaving medical information was kept from the two women who most needed that information. My friend, who loved Italy and had been there several times, was considering a life there. That experience gave her pause and ultimately she did not move to Italy.

As a woman, one must question whether one is willing to work within particular cultural constraints or if there is the will to overcome them and stand up for one's self. That is a question requiring a unique and individual answer.

So how does a woman find out about these cultural issues before making a move? Connect with women who are already living in these countries. There are usually online forums, Yahoo! groups and Facebook groups for each country she may be considering. Ask about the types of experiences the women there have had and find out how they've handled various situations. Sometimes it is less about sexism as it is about comfort levels on certain cultural norms.

For example: there are many countries where bribery is common. Getting a speeding ticket or getting items through customs can often end with an exchange of money-laden handshakes. Men tend to be more open to this behavior than women. I once had a man tell me that any time he was pulled over for speeding in Mexico, he'd just offer to buy the officer dinner. He suggested I do the same. Well, there was no way for me, as a woman, to make such an offer without it sounding like a date, or worse. And I wasn't sure that I wanted to be a part of bribery. So I needed to think about how I was going to handle that situation if it were ever to come up.

For some women, the cultural differences are a call to action. They see it as an opportunity to make a difference. I've met women who have started nonprofit organizations to help local women start businesses. There are women who work to end sex trafficking and others who work to improve education for local girls. For women whose hearts call them to be of service and change the situation for women in their new country, it's critical to create a support system that will be there through any uphill battles.

Another area of consideration is how a woman is perceived by the culture. Things she could get away with in her home country or as a tourist may not be acceptable as a local. If she wants to fit into the local culture, then it is polite to learn what the customs and behaviors are for women. Knowing how to behave can make a difference in how she is treated and how much respect she receives.

As an example, I have found that in Mexico women who are dressed, manicured, and have their hair perfectly done are often women of power. Dress equals status in Mexico and coming to a meeting in a t-shirt and shorts shows a lack of self-worth and certainly demonstrates a lack of consideration for others. This is especially true if the meeting is with one or more other woman. For example, if a woman is having trouble with the local Internet provider or a bank, arriving dressed in a fashionable power suit and looking her best will get her much further. After that, assuming she's dealing with another woman, the trick is to look her right in the eye and tap the desk with manicured nails while speaking. After a moment, there will be a telltale smirk from the woman behind the desk. That means the woman who has made the effort with her appearance and behavior has earned respect.

Lifestyle Choices

Women tend to have more requirements for the type of lifestyle they want. Guys can often be happy if they find a local pub that plays American sports on the television. Women need infrastructure and conveniences.

So the questions become, how easily can a woman live without a fancy salon to do her hair? How about trips to the spa? Shopping? Or maybe her interests are more outdoorsy. Like surfing? Or maybe hiking the trails or using a bike for daily chores? Each of these types of women will need to find cultures that can accommodate the life they want to lead.

If a woman is a city girl who likes pampering, then she should make sure that the cities she's considering have those extra amenities and that there are salons that will meet her nail, hair, and other personal care requirements. On the other hand, if she's the active outdoor girl, she needs to consider if the country will accommodate that with appropriate gear for women. Or are there cultural taboos around women and these activities?

Perhaps a woman's lifestyle needs revolve around church or philanthropy. Are there organizations in the area that will meet those needs? Often the needs of these types of groups are more important for women than for men. Women tend to need to build groups of likeminded individuals. So let's explore community for women living abroad.

Social Support Networks, Religious/Spiritual, Giving Back/Charitable Work

Women need the interaction of other women. Guys can drop into most any bar and find themselves other guys for sports talk or just general conversation. In many countries, that would be an invitation to men that would be extremely uncomfortable for a woman. There are exceptions though. Two women I know in Mexico opened a bar that, although it is open to everyone, caters to women. They have created a space that is safe and encourages women to drop in and strike up a conversation. So a woman shouldn't rule out that possibility. It just might require a bit of digging and conversation with other women to find those places.

Other ways for women to create community with other women is through local expat groups, online networks, hobby clubs, church groups, and charitable organizations. What's important is that women who are considering living abroad check out whether there are groups in the area she's considering that will meet her needs.

One great way to do that is to see if there are Facebook groups for a particular interest in the city being considered. One can search for them in English to find other expats who have similar interests. It's also possible to find groups of local citizens who like to do those things and it also allows one to improve language skills if the locals speak a different language. If there isn't a group, one option is for women to simply join a local expat group and ask if there's any interest in getting a group started. That could mean instant friends before even making a move.

Living Single, Dating & Sex

And speaking of making the move... what about being a single woman abroad? Being single and living in another country brings up some interesting situations that can be both fun and frustrating. Women, especially, need to be aware of cultural perspectives on dating. They need to understand how that culture looks at women from their home country. There can often be a belief that American women are rich and more willing to have sex. It's critical to understand how the local men view a single woman before she jumps into that dating pool.

Plus, what are the local dating beliefs? Is monogamy a given or is it considered normal for men to stray? Is it polite to look the man in the eye or does that indicate sexual availability in that culture? What are the taboos around single women and sex? If a woman dates within the local population, how can she be sure that the gentleman is single? Or is he interested in money or a ticket to the U.S.? And a woman has to decide if she's okay with that. It's not unusual for a man to move abroad looking for a wife so it is not uncommon for the local male population to assume that a single woman moving abroad just might be looking for a husband.

How does a single woman find out about all these interactions? She can seek out single women on the online forums and Facebook groups. It's then possible to contact these women privately to ask them what the dating situation is like and what the social mores are.

Health & Wellness

As was mentioned earlier, women's healthcare in certain countries can be influenced by the role of women in their society. One of the things a woman can do when visiting a potential location is to get a list of hospitals and doctors in the area that are recommended by other expats. If possible, she can get an appointment to meet with the doctor and find out his or her perspectives on medicine. Is their philosophy that the doctor is in charge or do they have a co-operative relationship with their patients? Most women will have a preference of one over the other.

Keep in mind that in most countries, one does not see commercials for prescription drugs that encourage one to "ask your doctor if this is right for you". The doctor will initiate any discussion about a specific drug. And this approach to TV and online advertising can suggest how much a doctor will allow a patient to be "in charge".

Sometimes this is a personal preference by the doctor, rather than a cultural norm.

For example: My friend Tammy bought an insurance plan with one of the local hospitals in Rosarito, Mexico and was very happy with her experience. However, she did notice that her doctor was very stoic and rarely explained much to her.

One day her primary care doctor was not available and she had to see a different doctor. This doctor couldn't have been more open. He explained her lab results in detail, gave her brochures on how to work with her condition, and was open to answering all of her questions. Tammy stayed with the hospital, but switched to this new doctor.

Of course, another area of medical concern for women is finding a good gynecologist for regular checkups and mammograms. Having a consistent doctor for those check-ups will make her much more comfortable in the event of a health concern. In addition, if she's single and planning to be sexually active, STD's don't stop at the border and they don't discriminate by age. So finding a doctor she can trust is essential.

There are directories online that identify doctors who have been certified through global health initiatives, an organization that seeks to create standards of care and treatment throughout the world. Doctors on the list have met those requirements. Of course, an excellent resource is women who are met through the local expat groups, in person or online. A private conversation with them will usually lead to the recommendation of a good gynecologist. Once a woman is established in her new home, local women she meets and becomes friends with are also very good resources.

Safety & Support

Women tend to have more safety concerns than men. Men are generally more concerned with property theft. Women need to know that their home is safe, that they can walk safely by themselves, or that they will have a supportive local community of women and friends who will go with them to events and make sure they get home safely. These are often subconscious acts that women do in their own country. In a new country, they will have an even greater need to make sure that those safety and support structures are in place as they acclimate to their new life.

When doing research before moving to a new country, women should be sure to check out the laws of the land. Do they have laws that support and protect women? Do they have governmental programs that create awareness on women's issues? If living in a city, are there call boxes and adequate police to create a safe environment for both men and women? And how good is the cell phone coverage and is there quick response to calls for help? It's important for women to know if they can call for help easily and for men, it's important to know if they will be able to provide the protection to others that good cell phone coverage offers.

In Baja, we have a system of call boxes along the toll road. If the car breaks down and a woman doesn't have a cell phone or there is no coverage, she can walk to a call box and a tow truck will come take her to safety. The cost of the tow truck is paid for by the toll. This is a safety precaution that, as a woman, I can really appreciate. There is nothing worse than being on the side of a toll road and not knowing where to go for help.

Another biggie for women is housing security. For some, gated communities or security camera monitored condos are the right fit. For others, a house in the country might be fine if it is equipped with a fence and a really big dog. Another consideration is whether the neighborhood has adequate lighting and if that lighting is maintained well. Sometimes in Mexico lights will go out on streets and the city won't replace them for up to a year. However, in the gated communities the lights are taken care of by the homeowners association. Thus, in local residential areas lighting may be iffy and in the gated community the area stays lit. Even when the local areas are safe, many women are not comfortable walking through their neighborhoods when it's dark and there are no lights.

That leads us to the topic of living among the locals versus living in private, mostly expat, communities. When I moved to Mexico, my initial thought was to live within the local community. However, I found that the safety and amenities of the gated communities were very enticing as a woman living alone. I was fortunate to find a gated community that has a mix of locals and expats and is located in the heart of Rosarito. This has provided me with the best of both worlds.

That is what this move is really about. It is about how a woman blends her old life into a new world. It is about making sure her needs to support her family can coexist with her desire to live abroad and that her cultural upbringing can mesh and grow in a new cultural environment. And, most importantly, that she can create the life she wants in a safe and healthy environment.

Just to review, the purpose of this chapter is to address many of the special requirements that women have when moving abroad. It's covered what some women and men have not considered or have not found in other books about living abroad. Use it as a guideline if you are a woman thinking of moving abroad. For men it can be used to make sure that any woman who is moving with him or who will be impacted by his move has their concerns addressed.

TRUST YOURSELF

CHAPTER TWELVE: IN CLOSING

OKAY, DEEP BREATH.

Did you notice that almost everything you've done with *The Happy Expat: Your Guide to Joyfully Retiring Abroad* has been focused on you? That most of the worksheets and questions have been asking you what you want and what seems best to you? Even if you just flipped through the book and thought about how you might answer some of the questions, you probably noticed that.

There's a reason.

When considering a decision that is as life changing as living abroad, it's critical that you make that decision for yourself. There is so much out there that will tell you where to live and give you a push in a particular direction. You are not thinking about this for someone else, you are doing it for you.

The most critical part of your decision is that it supports you and the life you want to live. What is right for me, for your best friend, for your siblings, may not be the right thing for you. Only you know the right answers for you.

And what's very cool is that now you have them!

You can make the choice that is right for you.

One of them might be that now is not the right time for you to follow this dream. Everyone must consider what is best at this particular moment in time and maybe "not right now" is your best choice. You can easily revisit this decision anytime you feel drawn to the idea of living abroad.

You have the tools to reevaluate your priorities and find the location that will provide what you need and want.

Another choice might be that you never live abroad. And you now know why. That means you can take it off your plate, cut yourself a break from continuing to struggle in that direction, and spend your new "free" time creating a different retirement life for yourself. What's very cool is that you have already figured out what you want that to look like and now you get to put it into place right where you are.

Your third choice is to move towards your dream of living abroad.

You have opened yourself to a way of life that you may have thought was impossible, all because you took the time to really think about so many things.

Look back at everything you've done and considered.

» Why do I even want to do something this crazy (or at least that's what a lot of my family and friends tell me)?

» Can I possibly afford to take off into the wild blue yonder (or, perhaps more importantly, can I afford not to)?

» What if I don't want to be gone all the time? Does it have to be all or nothing?

» What is so important to me that, even if I stay right where I am, I need to make sure is part of my life?

» How do I want my new lifestyle to look and feel and what do I need to make sure that's really possible?

» How can I keep my family and friends close to me without selling out on my dream?

» What about a foreign language or adapting to an entirely different culture or will there be anybody I will even like?

Yikes, there is just so much to do and find out...and, oh right, you've done a LOT of it already!

A word of caution before I send you off on your new adventure.

Let's say you do everything that has been suggested in this book – all the worksheets, research, charts, and read every word. Being this prepared does not mean there will be no glitches and no challenging moments that make you feel like you want to throw in the towel. What it means is that you've already thought through a lot of what will come up and you'll have a handle on how to manage your way through it. Plus, you've made connections with people like you who are living the life. They are an amazing resource, mostly because they have been where you are in your frustration and can offer some pretty solid advice. And because of all the work and thinking you've done, for those things that come up that you haven't already addressed, you now have the skills to figure it out and the confidence to do it.

Congratulations!

You have created a Framework that equals Freedom. Take hold of it with both hands and follow your dream.

Twenty years from now you will be more disappointed
by the things that you didn't do than by the ones you did do.
So throw off the bowlines.
Sail away from the safe harbor.
Catch the trade winds in your sails.
Explore.
Dream.
Discover. *

Wishing you all the best in your adventures, wherever they take you...
Ann

* H. Jackson Brown, Jr., *P.S. I Love You*

FOR WHAT IT'S WORTH

APPENDIX ONE: RESOURCES FOR RESEARCH

RESEARCHING YOUR MOVE ABROAD – WHAT YOU NEED TO KNOW AND how to find the best information

As you use the following resources, remember that it is up to you to bring a critical eye to everything you read and hear. The old adage "if something seems too good to be true, it probably is" should be kept in mind as you do any research. That being said, I have tried to give you quite a few places to begin your search. Some sites are repeated in two or more categories because they contain a wide spectrum of information.

Please don't limit yourself to the links or suggestions provided below. You know what is important to you and should make sure to learn as much as possible about those areas, in addition to the more common ones covered below.

A good first stop is http://www.enjoylivinginternationally.com. The blog will get your brain energized and you may read some tidbits you might not otherwise find. And sometimes those bits are what introduce you to a place you may never have considered before.

Getting started with general information

» http://www.nationmaster.com/ - this is a site to compare countries overall, be sure to look at more than one category; keep in mind that some countries will have little or no data and others will have a ton of data; also note the year given for the data & that there can be discrepancies from one set of data to another within the same country; this is not a perfect site and you should be looking at other sites as well – but it's a place to start

» http://travel.state.gov/content/passports/english/country.html - The following is the explanation used on this site to explain it's purpose: "We provide Country Specific Information for every country of the world. You will find the location of the U.S. embassy and any consular offices, information about whether you need a visa, crime and security information, health and medical considerations, drug penalties, localized hot spots and more. This is a good place to start learning about where you are going."

» https://data.oecd.org/ - this site looks primarily at Europe, plus a few countries south of the U.S., and a few outliers; what's nice is that you can see graphs and can add in another country to compare, e.g., France & the U.S. or France & Spain

Climate – weather for any city where data has been collected and averaged

» http://www.wunderground.com/history/ - be sure to notice what city is the basis for your information as it may be the city closest to the one you requested and not the city you actually entered in the search box, e.g., Tijuana instead of Rosarito, Mexico, even though Rosarito was the basis of the search

» http://www.nationmaster.com/country-info/stats/Geography/Climate - gives a very brief overview of country climate, not city specific

Healthcare

» http://www.who.int/gho/countries/en/ - this site looks at health data and statistics for lots of countries, it is not city specific; it's easy to get overwhelmed so just use it for getting an idea of healthcare for countries you are researching

» http://travel.state.gov/content/passports/english/country.html - once you enter your country of choice, you can then scroll to the Health tab and click the "+", again this is about the country not a specific location within the country

» For a specific location within a country, use your favorite search engine and enter the city and country of interest and add the word "healthcare" before you begin the search, e.g., Cuenca Ecuador healthcare. Click those links that seem most relevant to you.

» If you are curious about what health insurance might be available when moving abroad, use your favorite search engine and enter "worldwide health insurance". This will provide a fairly comprehensive set of results for the most widely used international healthcare insurance options. Check out several different sites as that will help you learn the various types of coverage. You can often learn just a bit more from the web site and you don't have to ask for a quote or give out your information unless you choose to.

Culture, Etiquette, and Politics

» http://www.countryreports.org/ - cultural, historical and statistical information on countries around the world. Downside – it is not free, although it is incredibly inexpensive. Click the Join link to get a quote.

» http://www.everyculture.com/ - again, an excellent all around site, with good coverage of culture and politics.

» http://www.executiveplanet.com/index.php?title=Main_Page - limited number of countries, still useful.

» http://culturebriefings.com/ - limited number of countries, must purchase, very inexpensive for the extent of information provided, click on "Purchase Culture Briefings", then on country of interest, and then scroll to bottom of that page to find out cost of that countries report.

» http://www.cyborlink.com/ - Although the number of countries is limited and this site is geared to business etiquette, dress, etc., it is helpful, as you will often find yourself in a business environment when dealing with utilities and other services.

» http://www.kwintessential.co.uk/resources/country-profiles.html - This site has very good information on basic etiquette for meeting and greeting someone, table manners, gift giving, business etiquette, plus more.

Safety – Please keep your common sense with you wherever you are, whether it's in your home country or abroad. In other words, don't check your ability to pay attention at the border, any border! I see it happen all the time and it can be uncomfortable and even dangerous for those who do.

» http://travel.state.gov/content/passports/english/country.html - Click on the Safety and Security "+". Just as the pamphlet you get with any prescription drug includes every possible reaction you could have, so does this coverage of this topic. It's all true and does not necessarily mean you will be faced with every situation discussed. Pay attention, make good decisions, and, for the most part, you'll be just fine.

» http://www.gov.uk/foreign-travel-advice - This is a UK source so that you can have another perspective.

» Use your favorite browser to find other information, e.g., "is it safe to live in xyz" (xyz is the name of the country or city & country of interest).

» I strongly urge you to verify any safety concerns you have with local expat groups for the location you are researching.

Financial – For many this is the driver they first consider. Use these links as guides and *always* be conservative as you look at your finances. It's better to end up with more money than you thought you'd have at the end of the day than to be scrambling to pay your bills.

> » http://www.finfacts.com/costofliving.htm - This site doesn't give you actual Cost of Living (COL) numbers (you have to pay for that). However, if you are willing to provide a little bit of information, you can see the list of how over 200 cities worldwide are compared to New York City using COL as the basis. Your city of choice may not be on this list but one in the near vicinity may be. For example, Quito, Ecuador is listed but Cuenca is not. So you can extrapolate from Quito that Cuenca is probably around the same if not a bit lower. The survey used measures the comparative cost of more than 200 goods and services in each location, including housing, transportation, food, clothing, household goods, and entertainment. To see that ranking, click on the link given above, scroll down until you see the blue highlighted link "Rankings". That will take you to the page where they ask you for information. Once you fill in the required items, click on the button below titled "See Rankings".

> » http://www.expatistan.com/cost-of-living - A rather cool tool. You can compare one city to another (if they have the data). Be sure to include the country because there are often cities with the same name in several different countries. For example, Cuenca is found in several countries so be sure to enter it as Cuenca, Ecuador or Cuenca, Spain, etc.

> » http://www.numbeo.com/cost-of-living/ - This site will give you some very basic information and then you need to give them an email address in order to get the more in-depth data. The numbers they show are based on having people who live in those specific places provide the data.

Buying or Renting Property

As I mentioned in the book, I urge you to rent first so that you can "try out" a place before committing yourself financially as you would if you bought a place.

That being said, here are some places to begin your search.

» Rental Property – For your first visit find a place that will be easy to live in. There will be so many things you want to see and do that spending your time figuring out how to turn on utilities can turn a fun experience into one that's less enjoyable.

   » http://www.wealthinformatics.com/ - In the search box at the top enter "avoid vacation rental scams" (without the quote marks) and press Enter. Then click the article titled "How to spot & avoid a vacation rental scam". This article should be read BEFORE you begin your search.

   » http://www.vrbo.com/ - This site has been around for a while so there are usually comments about the rentals offered.

   » https://www.airbnb.com/ - The difference between this site and VRBO is that these rentals are usually located in a private home. You will meet your host(s) and will have the opportunity to pick their brains about the location.

   » http://www.homeaway.com/ - This site has a lot of listings and a lot of reviews.

» Buying Property – This can be a wonderful experience, a horrible one, or something in between. In all good conscience I can't suggest any sites that I recommend to locate property for sale. I truly believe that the expat community is the best place to begin because they can recommend a trustworthy person to work with and a good lawyer. Keep in mind that how real estate is sold in the U.S. or Canada is not how it is sold in most other areas of our planet.

   » http://www.escapefromamerica.com/ - Click on the search

box and enter the words "real estate scams" (without the quote marks) and press Enter. This should bring up an article titled "Real Estate Scams to Avoid in Latin America". The information covered in this article can be applied outside of Latin America. As always, the guiding words are 'caveat emptor' – let the buyer beware.

» If you want to look around at what types of properties might be for sale in an area of interest to you, use your favorite search engine and enter the names of the city and country and then add "real estate for sale" (without the quote marks). If anything really catches your eye, get in touch with the expat community, provide a link to the property and ask if this is legit, if the price is reasonable, and if anyone can recommend a reputable agent and a lawyer who specializes in buying and selling real estate. And then proceed cautiously.

Language

Learning the language of where you're headed is a really good idea. You can either begin learning the basics before you go or after you get there. Knowing how to ask for directions, help with getting a taxi or using the bus, how much something costs, and ordering food would be very useful before you go, even if you plan to actually study the language after you get there.

» Online language sites – This is really tricky to recommend because we each have our own learning styles. Some sites are very visual, some are more word based, some provide a spoken way of learning, and some give you a bit of everything. It's important that you investigate each course to make sure it meets your criteria.

» http://fsi-languages.yojik.eu/ - This site is free and has a wide variety of languages to choose from. The courses were developed by the Foreign Service Institute and are "made available through the private efforts of individuals who are donating their time and resources to provide quality materials for language learning". They offer everything from Amharic to Yoruba.

» http://www.rosettastone.com/ - This is one of the premiere providers of non-classroom language learning. You can learn online or you can purchase CD's.

» http://www.babbel.com/?locale=en - Babbel has received good reviews and many have come to depend on their app as well as the online training they offer.

» If you want to find a specific language, you can also do your own search using the terms "learn Spanish online" (without the quote marks). Look for reviews of the business or organization behind the course. Be sure you understand what you are and are not getting before you hand over any money. Of course, if it's free, then you can stop using it and not be concerned you've wasted your money.

» Language schools

» If you want to learn a new language in a country where it is spoken, here are two ways to begin:

» Your best bet is to find out from the expat community living there if there are good language schools.

» Search the Internet for the language and location, e.g., "Spanish language school Cuenca Ecuador" (without the quote marks).

» If you want to begin learning a language before you go to the country and want a classroom experience, check with your local community college and local schools. Even if they don't have what you are looking for, they can often make suggestions for how to find what you want.

» Quick translation – When you see or hear a word or sentence you don't understand or are struggling with finding the words to say something, there are ways to work around that. The translation links below will at least get the idea across, sometimes better or worse than other times.

» https://translate.google.com/ - In the left hand block, click the language that you will be typing, type in the word(s) you want translated and in the right hand block click the language you want delivered. This site keeps you on the same page so you can continue to enter different words or phrases and it doesn't change pages.

» http://www.babelfish.com/ - Follow the Steps shown. For Step 3 click Translate in the lower right hand corner. This site will take you to another page when you click Translate. However, below the ads that will show up, you can enter a new word or phrase and again click Translate.

Country Rules / Regulations / Safety

» Paperwork & Documentation – This varies by country so it's important that you carefully research what you need to do.

  » An online search by country, e.g., "Argentina long term visa requirements for non-residents", will help you find a variety of resources to guide you as you research the documentation required by that country.

  » http://travel.state.gov/content/passports/english/country.html - This is another way to research what you need to do if you are considering living abroad. Enter the country of interest and click Go. You'll see a few helpful Quick Fact items. Then look below for the "Entry, Exit & Visa Requirements" bar and click it. This will give you a lot more information and also give you other links or information you need to consider.

» Shots & Medical Issues – You definitely want to know what's required and what might be happening medically anyplace you're considering.

» http://wwwnc.cdc.gov/travel - Enter your country of interest and click Go. There are five categories of information and take a look at all of them. Also, remember this is the Centers for Disease Control and it's their responsibility to cover as many possibilities as they can, even when there's only a remote chance you will be exposed.

» http://www.who.int/ith/en/ - The World Health Organization has a variety of links you will find useful. You can download various documents about vaccinations and other medical issues and there is also a report you can order that contains quite a bit of information.

» http://travel.state.gov/content/passports/english/country.html - Enter your country of interest and then click on "Health". This section covers what to expect health-wise and any other words of advice or caution about your health while traveling in the country discussed.

» Pets – if you are going for a short investigative trip, it would be best to take that first trip and find out all you can about what it's like to have a pet where you're considering living. If you can drive to where you're going, that will be easiest on your pets. If you can't drive, you will most likely have to fly your pets. If you do some investigation, you might be able to take them on a ship or freighter. However, you need to research all options carefully and talk with the vet who knows your pet(s) and can give you advice on what is the best option.

» http://www.pettravel.com/ - This site covers taking your pet(s) to quite a few countries by air. Start by clicking the "Pet Passports" tab at the top. You not only learn what the rules are about bringing a pet into your country of interest, you can also purchase a Pet Passport that will include all the documentation you need.

» http://www.petmovers.com/services/ - This is a business that actually moves your pets for you and walks you through every preparation step you are responsible for, including what paperwork you need and when. When the actual move occurs, they will keep you informed every step of the way.

Connecting with Expats

It will make a big difference if you connect with expats who are already living in your country of choice. Finding these groups can be easy or challenging. Regardless, you really should put in the time if you're serious because they can answer so many of your questions. They have all been in your shoes and walked the path of the new kid on the block. And your path will be smoother with their help.

Be sure to introduce yourself first and tell people what your interest is in their group. Please don't just start asking questions. You are unknown and they want to know a little about you before they start connecting with you. No life history here, just a simple hello, your first name, where you currently live (state/country is enough) and that you're interested in moving there.

» Expat Online Groups – You do not have to be a member to do your initial search of the following groups.

  » https://groups.yahoo.com/neo/dir/Cultures   Community/ Groups/Expatriates/ - To find expat groups, enter your country of interest followed by "expats", e.g., "Thailand expats". Then look through the results to find groups that might be useful to you. Once you get connected with one group, you'll find out about other groups.

  » http://www.transitionsabroad.com/ - Look on the left for the section labeled "Living Abroad" and then click on "Best Expatriate Resources". Then scroll down to the list of categories that are found in the middle of the page, below the photo. Click on "Expatriate Websites and Worldwide Portals". At the next page you see, scroll down and you will see a listing of a variety of websites. At the bottom of the page is a listing by country.

» Expat Online Groups – You can search without being a member. However, to be able to contact a group, you will need to signup.

  » http://www.meetup.com/ - In the search window enter your country of interest followed by "expats", e.g., "Panama expats". Be sure that you select "any distance" in the dropdown list to the right of the search box. You will then get a page that shows you the different Meet-Up groups that meet your criteria. When you click on a group, be sure to notice on the left where the group is located. You really want a group that is actually located in the country of interest. One in Minneapolis probably won't be very helpful to you. Then decide if you want to join a group and click Join us. You'll need to sign up with Meetup and then you can request to join the group.

» Expat Online Groups – You have to signup first before you can search for groups.

  » https://www.facebook.com - In the search window enter your country of interest followed by "expats", e.g., "Panama expats". While you are typing, Facebook will give you a dropdown list of different possibilities that seem related to your search. Click on one that interests you and then you can look at the page. If you like what you see, click the Join Group button. You have to be accepted into the group and then you can begin introducing yourself, reading through past comments, and asking your questions.

» Blogs – These are running commentaries about whatever the writer wants to share. Often excellent resources for everyday life, things to do, events that occur, and adventures that happen. Usually you can also contact the author.

» Use your favorite search engine and enter the country and "expat blogs", e.g., "Ecuador expat blogs" or include the city, e.g., "Cuenca Ecuador expat blogs". Select a blog and take a look. You'll see a variety of approaches to blogging so sit back and enjoy your reading.

Staying in touch with the folks back home – This often makes or breaks the success of living abroad. Two approaches to keeping the connection are blogs and actually talking with people.

» Set up your own blog, just as others have done. You can share what's going on in your new life. And you can do it when it fits your schedule. Then just make sure you give the URL for your blog to everyone you want to keep informed of your new adventure.

   » If you are not tech savvy, get one of your younger friends or relatives to get you set up and teach you how to use your new site.

   » If you are pretty knowledgeable about maneuvering through today's technology, then you can set up your own blog.

   » There are many free blogging sites. Since this is a constantly landscape, I'm not providing any direct links. Instead, use your favorite browser and enter "free blog sites" and you will find articles that review blog sites you can use for free. Plus, you'll also find links to several possibilities, e.g., WordPress, Blogger (a Google site).

» There are several ways you can talk directly with your friends and family. As the prices and coverage vary, you will need to do your research to find what is best for you.

   » https://www.facebook.com/

   » http://www.skype.com/en/

» http://www.magicjack.com/index.html

» http://www.vonage.com/

» And for those of you who use Apple devices, you can communicate worldwide with other Apple devices at no cost. FaceTime allows you to have a video conversation and iMessenger allows you to text.

THE END

APPENDIX TWO: CHAPTER TITLE CREDITS

- » Introduction – A Pirate Looks At 40…50…60… -- Jimmy Buffett (…50…60… added)
- » Chapter 1 – That's What Living Is To Me – Jimmy Buffett
- » Chapter 2 -- The Wanderer – Dion
- » Chapter 3 -- Money, Money, Money – Abba
- » Chapter 4 -- Don't Let Me Be Misunderstood – The Animals
- » Chapter 5 -- Changes In Latitudes, Changes in Attitudes – Jimmy Buffett
- » Chapter 6 -- Don't Stop Me Now – Queen
- » Chapter 7 -- This Must Be The Place – Talking Heads
- » Chapter 8 -- Family Affair – Sly and the Family Stone
- » Chapter 9 -- Got To Be Real – Cheryl Lynn
- » Chapter 10 -- Running On Empty – Jackson Brown
- » Chapter 11 -- I Am Woman – Helen Reddy
- » Chapter 12 -- Trust Yourself – Bob Dylan
- » Appendix 1 – For What It's Worth – Buffalo Springfield
- » Appendix 2 – The End – The Doors